Rapthology

LESSONS IN LIFE AND LYRICS

Wretch 32

WILLIAM HEINEMANN: LONDON

1 3 5 7 9 10 8 6 4 2

William Heinemann
20 Vauxhall Bridge Road
London SW1V 2SA

William Heinemann is part of the Penguin Random
House group of companies whose addresses can be
found at global.penguinrandomhouse.com.

Penguin
Random House
UK

www.penguin.co.uk

A CIP catalogue record for this book is available
from the British Library.

ISBN 9781785152009 (Hardback)

Typeset in 11.5/17.5 pt Quadraat Pro by Jouve (UK), Milton Keynes
Printed and bound in Great Britain by Clays Ltd, Elcograf S.p.A.

Penguin Random House is committed to a sustainable future
for our business, our readers and our planet. This book
is made from Forest Stewardship Council® certified paper.

MIX
Paper from
responsible sources
FSC
www.fsc.org   FSC® C018179

To everyone who came before me, and to everyone coming after. This is for you.

CONTENTS

INTRO: THE CRADLE

It's strange that as someone who's just written a book, I almost never put pen to paper when I'm writing lyrics. When you come into the studio with me, you'll find me pacing around. Mumbling words as the beat loops over and over. Half the time, what I'm saying doesn't even make sense. The verse takes shape as formless noises in my throat, snatches of phrases that fit, then back to the relentless sound. To my producer, to my sound engineer, it's all nonsense. But I'm working things out internally, editing something no one else can hear. Then in a moment, I'll have it – I'll run to the booth and lay down the verse. Metaphors, similes, puns and punchlines. If it's recorded, the words will stay in my head for ever. If I've forgotten it before I make it to the mic, it was never meant to be remembered in the first place.

You can hear music from before you're born. What your mum listens to, you listen to. But you're hearing it muted: like the sound is coming through water, through walls. Imagine if you could remember what that was like. Feeling the low rumble of bass, percussive thumps and bits of melody. And in the dark, there you are, trying to piece these patchwork sounds together, to hear the full song over the rapid rhythm of your own, brand-new heartbeat. It's only when you're born, when you emerge into the world with its glaring lights, its alien shapes and objects, that you can hear sound in all its sharpness. And at first, it's overwhelming. It's deafening. To find music again, you've got to learn what to block out as well as what to take in.

That's what it's like when I'm in the studio. I know that the song is out there, on the other side of some obstacle. But it's muffled, it's half formed, it's not quite solid. It's like what I can see are the blurred shadows of what it is I'm trying to grasp. And then sometimes when an idea comes, it's too much. The beat and the lyrics are at war, yelling over one another to tell the story. Maybe the melody's trying to dominate everything else; perhaps the bass is cracking your rib as it tries to make you move. The song you've got isn't art yet: you've got to refine it, with the tools and techniques you have at your fingertips. You've got to chip things away, as well as tack them on.

This book is about how you develop those tools and techniques. What is it that you need to apply to an idea to turn it into art? More fundamentally, who is it you need to be in order to write a song? Each time you create a verse, you're rewriting who you are. You've put a bit of yourself out there for the world to have. Everyone knows that Shakespeare said, 'All the world's a stage', but people forget the part that follows: 'And one man in his time plays many parts.' This is the story of the parts I've played in my life – a schoolboy, a soldier, a father – and how these stages of man made me an artist. I've never really been one for drama though: this is a *Rapthology*, a life told through lyrics.

If what you're after is a celebrity memoir, full of glitter and sleaze, then you've got the wrong book. Put it down, pick up another one. I'm not a gossip columnist; I'm a lyricist. What you learn about me in this book is never intended as a shock revelation. Everything I tell you is in service of songwriting.

You'll hear about my experiences of loss, success, love and heartbreak because those have been the ingredients of my work. *Rapthology* is a lesson by example. I'm showing you how you can approach life to turn it into art. Once you've been affected by something, you can store the emotion that you need to pull an idea from the other side of that wall and into reality. You can own it, control it, put it into words and lift the weight off your shoulders by putting those words out into the world.

The lyrics themselves are lessons on life. They draw from things that I've directly experienced, and are expressions of my world view. I'm never trying to preach from on high, but I do want to share my perspective on family, politics, culture and coming up in the school of hard knocks. I never got to learn things the easy way.

There was never a book to guide me through it – maybe *Rapthology* can be yours. In it, you'll learn everything they don't teach you in the classroom. But I don't just want you to follow in my footsteps. Education is a failure if the student only ever gets as good as the teacher. I want my readers to be inspired to write; to do what I do, and then do it better.

You'll learn about some of the commercial concerns in making music too. I look at artists like clothing. An artist has to decide what kind of shop they'll be. Are you going to be H&M? Are you going to be Zara? Are you going to be D&G? How are you going to balance being high end with being able to attract enough of a customer base to keep you afloat? You might be the new brand that everyone wants for a while. There are fake versions of you everywhere. And then all of a sudden, no one wants to wear you. Overnight, you go from being a fad to being forgotten. Whereas the person wearing the Levi's 501s is still wearing them. If you have a shop on Oxford Street, you could sell 100,000 items a week. When you move, you could sell 100,000 a year, but you're committed to the art. Not everything is going to appeal to everyone. I'm going to teach you about the difference between mass production and craftsmanship.

You'll hear about the combination of instinct and intellect that I had to utilise in order to become known as 'your favourite rapper's favourite rapper'. Every single baby is born with the natural urge to communicate. But to achieve language takes learning, and to become Shakespeare takes training. I'm treating my lyrics in this book the way literature gets treated in an anthology. Why? Because they deserve it. Some of the techniques that I show you come from the Ancient Greeks and Romans; others are my own inventions. I'll break down songs bar by bar, sometimes even syllable by syllable, to show you how much thought has gone into something that looks effortless.

This book will take you from the cradle to the coffin, on a journey of my work from forgotten gems to greatest hits. You'll learn about my philosophy on life and my definitions of art. By showing you how my mind works, I want you to end up with a similar understanding of yourself. Both writers and readers observe the lives of others, even if that means looking at your own life through the eyes of a stranger. *Rapthology* is the story of how writing stops you from being a victim of your own experience, and turns you into a viewer of it. Over the next seven chapters, I'm going to show you that by surrendering to art, you become a victor over life.

I.

THE SCHOOLBOY
('PUNCTUATION', 'PISCES')

Then the whining schoolboy, with his satchel
And shining morning face, creeping like snail
Unwillingly to school.

Punctuation

I'm levels above that's blatant
Just check my punctuation
I'm coming to take it run with the game
None under the sun's adjacent
I'm levels above that's blatant
Just check my punctuation
I'm coming to take it run with the game
None under the sun's adjacent

Capital letter who's better than Wretch over
here or close
Who's had an exceptional year not most
Who's actually sped through the gears or drove
question mark
You guys ain't moving step up your level

I'm underground with the heat the Devil the street
   the ghetto the scene (huh) who's hot full stop
After I slept with talent I divorced my nerves
And my mixtape it recorded my birth
Of course I'm preferred check my verbs
The heat starts when my speech marks (Yeah)
When they cut the cord then I knew I must
   perform
My worst bar's way above the norm
And that's no estimation exclamation
New paragraph each time I write
Screw managers they just want a piece of the pie
You'd think they knew I move food
By the way they wanna eat of my lines
Comma look I can see through my eyes
I can hear through my ears
I don't wanna get locked 'cause I'm fearing the years
Comma I'm already behind bars

I'm levels above that's blatant
Just check my punctuation
I'm coming to take it run with the game
None under the sun's adjacent
I'm levels above that's blatant
Just check my punctuation
I'm coming to take it run with the game
None under the sun's adjacent

(Look) Who's better than Wretch over here full stop
Who's had an exceptional year question mark
I'm the greatest exclamation quotation
Who's better than Wretch over here full stop
Who's had an exceptional year question mark
I'm the greatest exclamation quotation

New paragraph capital I I'm gonna capitalise and
    capture my hype
I'm that it's my time comma you slack in your prime
    full stop
(Look) Let me roll on semi-colon you're a waste
    of time
Space line paper so in brackets I'm greater
No hyphen (huh) and you won't forget me if you
    remember the titans
My writing stays at the highest peak I ride the beat
I won't fall off I like my seat quotation so hot so
    blatant
I won't stop no patience is left in me I'm blessed indeed
    I'm next excuse me
I got manners I'm polite G
Even though I've got manors behind me
Like T that's abbreviated slightly
Will I be the greatest likely I might be
Dash high percentage that's just my perspective plus
    my Wretchrospective

I'm levels above that's blatant
Just check my punctuation
I'm coming to take it run with the game
None under the sun's adjacent
I'm levels above that's blatant
Just check my punctuation
I'm coming to take it run with the game
None under the sun's adjacent

(Look) Who's better than Wretch over here full stop
Who's had an exceptional year question mark
I'm the greatest exclamation quotation
Who's better than Wretch over here full stop
Who's had an exceptional year question mark
I'm the greatest exclamation quotation

Your school years are when you really work out who you are. You step through those gates and you've entered a laboratory. Experimenting through combinations – different kinds of people, kinds of conversation, testing yourself against teachers – and seeing what comes out of your character. By the time you leave, you'll know whether you're the kind of person who swims along with the school, or the kind who goes against the current.

I knew from the start that I wanted to go my own way. My older sisters were a pair, and they were at secondary school together. Both of them went to Langham, but I went to Northumberland Park; even to this day, I'm not entirely sure why. Maybe it was me wanting to stand alone. Or be unconventional. Everyone's expecting me to go to one place, so I go somewhere else. Everyone's wearing yellow, so I wear red.

I always had confidence, growing up. There was no one I wouldn't speak to at school. I was the person trying to make everyone feel comfortable. It's like, if there were a few of us walking down the corridor together, and there'd be one boy on his own, walking towards us, who was a bit shy, I'd always say something to them before anyone else had a chance to. Just, 'We've got maths later, yeah? See you there.' So no one would say something cheeky or rude. It was never a big thing.

You've got to tap into that underdog energy if you wish to reciprocate it. On one hand, rap is about being the best, braggadocio, bigging yourself up. But you're only going to make it as an artist – someone who's really got something to say – if you have the guts to stick your neck out and do something a bit different. That might come at a social price at school, but out in the world it's going to be your pay packet. Find what makes you different, and refine it. No one remembers the guy who never strays beyond the centre of the pack.

School was the time I worked out what that thing was for me. I mean, I always had an imagination. Reading, writing, comprehension – these were the things which came quite naturally to me. The kids' books we got given early on didn't hold my attention. My mum would read me a book about Biff and Chip or whatever, and I'd come away dissatisfied. I just didn't think they were very good stories. It was underwhelming, and I suppose that got me thinking about whether I could write something better.

I remember when I was younger a social worker came round to interview me. And even at that age, I could tell what it was they wanted to hear. Trauma, drama, tears. So I just started making stuff up – telling really outlandish tales, drawing pictures with blood and guts, all kinds of fucked-up shit. They must've thought I was a little psycho! But I wasn't acting out because of any deep inner pain – it was because I knew even then that people prefer the vivid colours of a story to the dreary ones of real life.

It wasn't until I arrived at Northumberland Park that I realised I wanted to put my mind to more than just winding up Haringey Council's finest. The person who helped me identify that I had something slick was my English teacher Mr Henry. (Ghetts actually got taught by him as well.) I'd never been made to feel like I was smart by other teachers. Mr Henry had a way of helping you realise you already understood the thing he was trying to teach you. Other teachers might say you'd got an answer wrong only because you didn't explain it in the exact way they wanted, and as a kid you end up doubting what you thought you'd actually got your head around – 'Hang on a minute, maybe I *don't* get it.'

But Mr Henry understood that students comprehend things in different ways, and he went out of his way to make me see that I knew what I was talking about. If he'd ask a question in class and I said I couldn't explain the answer, he'd pick up my exercise book and show me where I'd actually demonstrated the thing I'd just said I didn't know. If you tell a kid they're ignorant, then obviously they'll just go away thinking they're ignorant. But if you show them the full scale of what they could understand unconsciously, they'll be able to do it again by themselves. And a hundred times out of a hundred, they'll get the answer right when they're asked the question again.

Mr Henry was the first to show me that the way I write is worth something. And that's such a powerful thing when you're at school. When a teacher has faith in your abilities, you feel like a champion. I only had him as a teacher until Year 9, but he was such a key figure for me. Neither me nor Ghetts have been able to forget what he did for us. When we speak about Mr Henry, Ghetts will say the same thing: that he was able to see something special in the kids other teachers would dismiss out of hand. I guess you could say that Mr Henry is one of the biggest unsung heroes in the Tottenham grime scene.

It was in his lessons that I learned that good writing is a combination of instinct and intellect. You definitely need both. There are writers who are technically perfect – everything is immaculately researched, they've assessed a million times how each syllable could be interpreted by the reader – but the work is still no good. It doesn't have any soul in it. You have to develop a feel for writing, like those cooks who judge by touch and taste without having to measure a single ingredient. Even today, writing this book, there are times I can't tell you why I made a decision to use a certain word or phrase. There's just a sensation that comes over you when you find the right thing to say, like slotting a puzzle piece into place. But without intellect, your vocabulary is going to be too limited to be able to find that perfect phrase. You're trying to paint a picture when you've got half the palette missing.

I got something like a B and two Ds in my GCSEs, but honestly I really enjoyed English. The problem with being put in a Foundation class – where you can't be graded any higher than a C – is that it robs you of ambition. One of the worst things you can do to a kid is set a low bar and say, 'I don't believe you're capable of anything better than this.' It's crushing. So I ended up not doing my coursework, which really annoyed my teacher Ms Collinson, because it would have helped my overall mark. We had a bit of a weird relationship. She knew I was funny and I was good with words, but couldn't understand why I didn't just apply myself.

The lessons where I did really well were when we got to do more than just explain what was in front of us. So maybe Ms Collinson would read a poem out at the beginning of the class, but instead of just sitting and taking notes, we had to write our own poems on the theme. I liked it when we got to rework things ourselves, to reimagine what a story was and inject our own perspectives. It woke up a little bit of competitive instinct in me. I always wanted to better what I had to study through what I was able to create. I had to have something to beat. I suppose it was similar for rapping – I'd hear a song, and want to squeeze my own lyrics into any bar which didn't have vocals on it.

Poetry and rap come from the same family. They're brothers. Just because you're good at one doesn't necessarily mean you'll be good at the other, but if you master both you'll be unparalleled. In some ways, writing a rap is more difficult. If you choose, you can write a poem in free verse, without metre or rhyme. But with rap you're always writing your lyrics to a specific rhythm, and usually one that's been composed by somebody else. Your speed is dictated by a tempo. It's like you have to find a way to breathe while your chest is being tightly constricted: you have to develop special techniques to inhale and exhale the same amount of air that another person could do without thinking.

The most creative work is almost always trying to find a way around a barrier or rule of the artist's own making. Without restrictions, how do you know when you're pushing yourself? If I say that I'm going to run thirty miles, it makes a difference if I say I've got ten hours or twenty-four hours to run it in. (I'm probably not even running it in that time!) But if I say I'm going to run thirty miles in under four hours, that will put the fire up me. When you have a tight frame to operate within, it takes more skill to do well. Think about it: there's no high jump without a bar, and it works the same way for music. Power is about operating within and around that which constrains you.

I've always liked the thought of doing a song which is like an experiment. When I think of someone who's a clever writer – like Swiss – I'm always curious about what they could do on a track that's got restrictions. I've said to Swiss before: let's do a tune where we have to pick the words the other person can use. So maybe I choose 150 words, and that's all he can use for his verse. Or maybe he puts a limit on how many times I can use a particular word. But I've not fully convinced him yet – he's always like, 'Sounds a bit long, mate.' Maybe someone like Akala might be interested, I don't know.

That's why I enjoy writing with concepts. Some people can just write a song about nothing, no choruses, take the paper and go. And I'm not saying I can't write like that, but I like sticking to a topic. Because when you write like that, you're setting yourself a challenge – how many sick sentences and sick rhymes can you pull out of a break-up? It sets off a train of thought. What else breaks? There are break-ups, breakdowns, things that break that you can fix, things that break that you can never replace. It's not just people that break up either, so maybe I start talking about enzymes . . .

If I'm honest, I can't really categorise myself as an artist. I always wanted to go where my wind was blowing. Hundreds of years ago, there were poets who wrote like that too. Called metaphysical poets, they thought that how something is said out loud is more important than how you read it on a page. So they'd take a word like 'Sunday' and squeeze all the meaning out of just that sound – sun, son, soon. It sounds a bit obvious now, though I'd throw in a Capri-Sun reference just to shake it up a bit. The metaphysical poets were able to demonstrate that flexibility exists even where language seems incredibly fixed and limited. It's like being a chef. Ultimately there's a finite number of ingredients that exist in the world, but there are infinite ways of putting dishes together, drawing out new flavours by blending unexpected combinations. It's the same with language: you're working with material that existed long before you came into the world, and your task is to find something new in the seemingly obvious. I like how the metaphysical poets always went back to the way words sounded to find a double meaning. It's like trying to see the individual trees, and not the forest in front of you.

I personally found grime as a genre quite restricting. When I started out, writing very rigidly in that way, I noticed that my mum and my auntie and my older sister would listen to my stuff but didn't really get it because it was too fast. And it used to bother me so much! I would get so frustrated, because it doesn't matter what I'm writing about, you should be able to understand it.
I had to change my sound. I had to understand that there always has to be a point of difference between you and your competitors. If there are ten shops on the high street, there's gonna have to be a special reason for why you walk into any particular one. We all have that one corner shop that we stuck with growing up. Didn't matter if the others next door would chop and change, we'd stick with our guy. And his point of difference is that he's friendly, he's been there the longest, he always knows what you're gonna get. Whatever it is, he makes you feel like you've got a connection there. And that's how I write my songs. I want to make music that everyone can listen to, but the reason why you'll come to me first is because I'll write concepts better than anyone else.

'Punctuation' is the first song I did where I took a concept and tried to deliberately push it as far as it could go. Before that, I was in the stage of just developing the skill of wordplay. Nothing was fully fleshed out. At the time 'Punctuation' came out, there was a formula in music: catchy hook, repeat your verse, aggressive beat, keep it simple. But for me that was too easy – it didn't feel like an achievement to swim with that stream. So I knew 'Punctuation' had to be the one we put the effort into promoting, that we shoot the video for. A lot of people were against the idea. They said I had easier songs to listen to: 'That's not a radio song, it's not a song that will get you bookings.' But I reasoned that it's better to have a signature song than a booking song. If you want to intrigue people at an all-white party, walk in wearing red. It's not a one-off thing, either – you'll ensure your longevity if you stand firm and alone rather than falling as a group.

Working with concepts is hard to pull off. You're trying to take something that's already a metaphor and chop it up, rework it, and expand it into its fullest form. You're constantly trying to tread the line of being creative without losing your audience – because after a certain point, they'll get bored if all you can do is be slick without having something more to say.

The theme of that whole mixtape was *Teacher's Training*. It was my second mixtape: the first one was called *Learn from My Mixtape* and the cover was just A4 lined paper. I was already interested in the theme of taking you back to school: setting myself up as the teacher, and it's my life experience that you learn from. I guess I was looking for a cool concept about education for people who might have dropped out of school. I sat down to think about a lesson, and obviously maths wasn't gonna work; I don't know enough about science without googling; so I came back to punctuation. It felt natural.

Everything under the sun's been done, never forget that. So the challenge for an artist is taking something old and making it sound – and feel – new. In 'Punctuation', I'm turning out the rapper's bread and butter: it's all braggadocio, saying, 'I'm the best.' That's the constraint in which you have to show your power – no one can claim to be the best rapper if they say it in those exact words. What distinguishes you from your peers is being able to say something everyone's heard before, in a way that no one's heard before.

Throughout the track, I'm directing your attention to what makes my work different. Because I'm inviting the listener to 'check my punctuation', I'm letting them know that the delight is in the details. Not all of the images are to do with spelling and grammar either. If I'd stuck rigidly to one set of imagery, the song would have turned out clunky and linear – there wouldn't have been any surprises. But that's just not how I write.

For me, a bar is like a Rubik's cube, and each word I choose is a turn of the cube. The point of each twist is that you've changed the bar, so it's not just a repetition of the last thing you said, but you know there's a right direction and a wrong turn. So in the lines 'After I slept with talent I divorced my nerves / And my mixtape it recorded my birth', I'm playing with the idea of a life cycle in reverse. I took the idea of sleeping with something at the start – and then I'm thinking maybe I've caught something, or something's born out of that, there's marriage and divorce. But I could've gone down another route and talked about going to sleep and never waking up, dreams and nightmares, sleep is the cousin of death . . .

You have to let the resonance of words work on you. When you think about 'Punctuation', using correct grammar and all that, you start thinking about decorum – and that's how I get to 'I got manners, I'm polite G / Even though I've got manors behind me'. It takes the concept to an unexpected place – I'm able to juxtapose two contradicting ideas, of me being the polite boy who has the streets to back him up. If you were flipping through the thesaurus looking for synonyms of the word 'punctuation', you'd never have arrived at that image. It's important not to be too literal when you're working with concepts.

One of the most exciting things about rapping is when you realise each word has the potential to take you off in a wild direction. Each turn of the Rubik's cube opens up a million new routes for your imagination. Me and Avelino play this game with each other all the time. So if I say I was in a session with Wayne Hector, he'll go, 'Oh, L'il Wayne Hector?' Then I'll say, 'Wayne Hector Bellerin', and we just keep going and going until both of us are laughing and can't talk any more. It's the exact same game when you're writing a song: you're just playing, turning things around until all the colours match up and you have the perfect little cube.

Looking back on 'Punctuation', there are obviously things I might do differently today – a little brush-up here, a little clean-up there. But if there are ten reasons why I've been here since 2006, that track's one of them, without a doubt. It opened up so many doors (and ears) for me! I'd do interviews and be asked relentlessly about it. Because it made people interested in my process, more than in just the record itself. And that's so important to learn. The songs are always gonna come and go, but if they care about how your mind works you've automatically got longevity. It's the difference between having a character and just relying on a gimmick.

It helped me get to know myself. There are so many little techniques in that song which I refined later in my career – like letting one image turn into another, and another, but holding it all in the same bar. That becomes my signature for something like a Fire in the Booth. But it also gave me the room to be weird.

Pisces

Listen, I've got my head above water
I can approach your boat
But I just H2O the flow
I'm the captain of the ship that you cruise behind
I get deep like a scuba line, the ink splashes
Still, my notions are crystal clear
I'm the closest you've been to air, I'm an ocean
So my dome never overflows
I surf the waves, I ain't known to row
When I'm rhyming
Woo, it's like I'm on my own island
I'm getting fed up of you pirates
I'll write on palm trees and spit at your eyelids
And maybe you'll see what I'm saying
So current, it's the sea that I lay in
No covers, no others are original
I'm honoured cuh I'm lyrical
My inner thoughts say my life's guarding my spiritual
The ink splashes out, I don't think at all

My brain waves with the tide
So they will not be on my wavelength
I say bye
They'll be looking at me waving
Fishes

Only the tide's on my wavelength
Witness
Me saying bye cuh
I wave with the tide
So they will not be on my wavelength
I say bye
They'll be looking at me waving
Fishes
Only the tide's on my wavelength
Witness
Me saying bye cuh
I wave with the tide

I've got a head above water
I'm getting fed up of piranhas
Cuh they're tryna bite at the Pisces
You're tryna blow
But I'm the hurricane to your light breeze
The seaweed's getting to the heads of these might-bes
Slightly
But I'm as certain as a person can be
I'm on another wave, you're just surfing on me
Myspace is terrific
But as long as you know, Myspace is your limit
And for sailors that wanna test the water
This is infected, your O2 will get disconnected
No airtime, drown in your cells

Get afloat or bow to the whale, that's a killer
The guy who done the moonwalk was my idol
Now you're looking at the guy that walks on the tidal
Wave, my sky's all grey
Cause Michael strayed but I walk straight

My brain waves with the tide
So they will not be on my wavelength
I say bye
They'll be looking at me waving
Fishes
Only the tide's on my wavelength
Witness
Me saying bye cuh
I wave with the tide
So they will not be on my wavelength
I say bye
They'll be looking at me waving
Fishes
Only the tide's on my wavelength
Witness
Me saying bye cuh
I wave with the tide

Got my head above water
As a boy, I wished to float
Cuh I used to skim them stones

Like you, but the lighthouse put the spotlight on me
I'mma shine now, it's a lot now, I'm deep
I mean, I've been writing in navy blue
I'm inspiring, I rate my moves
That's passion
As a boy, the mega drive was to echo the dolphin
And now I wear Ecko on clothing, that's fashion
(Listen to my flow) imagine
No waves in my hair
Still I flow like there's waves everywhere
There's a lot of ink splashing on my page, I'm aware
But that's me venting my thoughts
I'mma ride with the tide till I'm dead on the shore
I'm surfing, cuh I know I flows
That's for ever living on the water surface, I float
So (listen to my flow)

My brain waves with the tide
So they will not be on my wavelength
I say bye
They'll be looking at me waving
Fishes
Only the tide's on my wavelength
Witness
Me saying bye cuh
I wave with the tide
So they will not be on my wavelength

I say bye
They'll be looking at me waving
Fishes
Only the tide's on my wavelength
Witness
Me saying bye cuh
I wave with the tide

Wave with the tide
Wave with the tide

It's a shame it never got the love it deserved, but 'Pisces' is one of my favourites. If 'Punctuation' tells you about what I'm capable of, 'Pisces' tells you how my mind works. It was mad fun to write. I tried to think about everything associated with water. I knew I had to be delicate with this one – I was laying back, relaxed, listening to atmospheric sounds. It was like I was trying to put myself in the mindset of a submarine, trying to recreate a full sensory experience. The only thing I could've done more is write this song on a ferry!

This is really important: I've talked about how poetry and rap are from the same family, but the main dividing line is that as a rapper I have the ability to use sound to shape meaning. Think about the difference between reading a script and watching the film: all the elements like setting, pace, volume, sound effects are pulled out from your imagination and brought to life all around you. Getting the production right involves as much technique and skill as rhyming. You want it to stir up emotions without drowning out your words – it's a fine tightrope to walk, sweeping the listener along with the music while making sure they're alert to what you're saying.

'Punctuation' was the song that took me places, but 'Pisces' is where I'm trying to take you somewhere. In 'Pisces', I'm trying to build a sensory deprivation tank. You're meant to be floating, and all you can hear is what I've chosen to play you. I wanted people who'd heard 'Punctuation' to hear 'Pisces' and know that it wasn't a fluke. I want my listeners, for however long the song is, to feel immersed in water. You're on a beach, you're in a submarine, or maybe you're a fish in the ocean. It's said that just before you drown you experience peace unlike anything else you can experience in life. And in a strange sort of way, this song is taking you to that place of deep water. The whole song is meant to feel meditative. We used splashes instead of drums; we put dolphins and seagulls on the track to really transport you. You're meant to feel like you're alone on the prow of a ship, just drifting with the current. I was expecting everyone to go nuts for this one, like it was the moment the ball was gonna drop and I'd get a knighthood or something! But it stayed a bit more of a hidden gem. There's an irony there – I was the only one on my wavelength.

If I made that exact same song today, I would create even more of a wrap-around experience. I'd shoot the video in a submarine, or maybe even bring a select number of people into an aquarium of my own design. I'd choose all the species of fish, and create an aquatic landscape of screens and speakers under the water. There's always a bit of a control freak in an artist: all I want to do is show you how to enjoy the music. Again, it's a bit like being a chef: you don't just serve people the meal in a restaurant, you give them the cutlery and plate to eat it off as well. Nowadays with social media it's quite easy to do that. I can film myself in my car listening to a new song, or do an Insta story breaking down an idea. If you're making a club song, you can tease it by sharing content where your tune is playing in a party setting. It's laying the groundwork for how you want people to experience the music when it's out. It's a whole new avenue for creativity. All the stuff around a song helps a conceptual writer like me.

I guess that mood of drifting along sits a bit odd with people. It's not meant to stir up strong emotions like 'Antwi' or bamboozle you with skill like with 'Punctuation'. The sound is just not what you expect from grime – it's not that 140 bpm, glitchy kind of vibe.

When you listen to something like Wiley's *Treddin' on Thin Ice*, you can hear the environment where it was made. It sounds like a concrete jungle. But 'Pisces' is just this really wavy soundscape. I made the track knowing it would swim against the current of the classic grime template: everyone was expecting aggression and hype, but I wanted to create a different kind of texture. Something which really drew from my unconscious mind.

There's always been something at the back of my brain drawing me towards water. I suppose that's because I'm a Pisces – which itself is a bit of a contradiction, because I can't swim. My spirit pulls me to the sea, while my legs tell me to run away! Water, at its most basic level, represents flow to me. It's like a liquid chameleon, capable of changing seemingly at will. It can be still enough to skim stones on, or it can crash against rocks with enough force to break them apart. We call our planet 'Earth', but most of it is covered by water. I mean, we call ourselves 'human', but most of us is made up of water too. We all rely on it to live, but we can't live in it. There are parts of the oceans which are more mysterious to us than the surface of Mars. I suppose the depth of the sea represents the depth of creativity I can draw from. It's limitless, just like an artist should be.

★

Writing to a concept means you're pursuing depth over breadth. It's not about running from Thornton Heath to Timbuktu in the space of three minutes; it's about drawing up water from a deep well, and making sure it tastes fresh with every sip. It's like trying to draw a spiral where you can always see the centre of the whirl: you're someplace new and unexpected, but never lost at sea. If the production of 'Pisces' is like a sensory deprivation tank, the lyrics are the hallucination you have while floating inside. 'My brain waves with the tide' isn't just a pun on brainwaves – it's a whole pattern of thinking. I'm trying to paint a picture rather than tell a story: across the verses, words and phrases connect up in different ways, with meaning as fluid and slippery as water itself.

The song starts out with classic braggadocio, this time using water imagery. I'm embodying all the elements of the sea at once: 'I've got my head above water' but I can also 'get deep like a scuba line'; I'm in the ocean and can 'approach your boat' but I'm simultaneously 'the captain of the ship that you cruise behind'. Even though the genre is similar to what I do in 'Punctuation', there's something different going on here. And to understand it, you have to turn to poetry to get your head around the technique.

When you're reading a poem, one of the first things you ask is 'Where is the poet in this piece?' You work out whether the poet is speaking as themselves, or adopting a character. Are they narrating in the third person, and trying to be objective, or are they telling you something in the first person, with an agenda at work? Are they talking to you, the reader, directly, or are they speaking to someone in particular? Writing in verse, whether it's poetry or rap, means developing one voice that can speak in many voices at once. And it's up to your audience to work out if they mean any of the things they say.

So in 'Pisces', even though my voice is consistently delivering braggadocio, it's diffused across the verse. It's like my spoken self is dissolved in the sea, and can manifest itself through contradicting similes and motions. In literature, this style is called *elliptical* poetry, where the poet conjures up a persona to speak the poem, but employs verbal tricks to make it so that the spoken selves aren't ever just one thing. That's my voice in 'Pisces' – I can move through different forms so that you never feel you've truly got a grip on me. I'm like water, slipping through your fingers.

To keep the lyrics moving, it was really important that I pushed myself to find words which didn't have stable meanings. Because when you've been rapping long enough, you're capable of writing a song in a few minutes. You follow a simple formula: beat, bars, hook, repeat. But if you're going to be great, you have to strive beyond just being capable. Capable isn't going to be what provides you with the best song – or maybe it does in one track out of a hundred. You must reach for the words which don't come to your grasp so easily. It's something I go on about to Avelino all the time: he has the talent to write a verse in three minutes, but if he spends thirty minutes exploring every potential avenue before he settles on the final product, it's going to be something special.

For 'Pisces', that meant finding words that were reactive. It's like when you're in a science lesson, and you've got a piece of potassium or something that's going to burst into bright flames on contact with water. Take a section like

> I'm getting fed up of piranhas
> Cuh they're tryna bite at the Pisces
> You're tryna blow
> But I'm the hurricane to your light breeze
> The seaweed's getting to the heads of these might-bes

First, I'm setting up an image of the rap game like it's an episode of Blue Planet – I'm the Pisces swimming against the current, and everyone else is trying to kill me. It's a fish-eat-fish world out there! But the word 'bite' has the double meaning of 'copy' there too, so a layer of meaning is added: I'm under attack by people who aren't capable of creativity themselves, who want to copy my style.

So then we're talking about competition and success. I'm addressing my rivals now, saying, 'You're tryna blow', as in they're all hoping to make it as big. But instead of using the more common phrase of 'blow up', I chop off the second word, so it carries implications of exhaling rather than just exploding. And because of that one simple choice, I have the freedom to move on to the next bar – if we're talking about who's got the capacity to blow, me versus other rappers is like a hurricane against a light breeze. Even that comparison isn't entirely straightforward: a hurricane isn't just a tropical storm, it's an alcoholic drink made with two kinds of rum. It's strong – much stronger than a sea 'breeze', which is mostly juice. So I'm not just saying I'm powerful like a storm, but that I'm potent like a hurricane. And because of that little hint of intoxication there, I can bring in the 'seaweed' pun at the end: these rappers going against me must be high!

That's the irony of the song. Even though I'm announcing to you that my process is instinctive ('The ink splashes out, I don't think at all'), every word choice is deliberate and thought over. If I'd said 'eat' instead of 'bite', 'blow up' instead of 'blow', or 'cyclone' instead of 'hurricane', that whole section wouldn't work. It's hinged on the littlest things. There's an Italian word for working like this: *sprezzatura*. It means that when you make art or literature, you disguise the effort and agony that went into making it. A song is meant to be like a swan gliding on top of the water. You don't see the feet paddling like mad underneath.

It's funny that in 'Pisces' you never hear me say the phrase 'it's funny'. Or I suppose it's ironic that I never use the word 'irony'. I've noticed that those are my go-to words that I draw on when I'm talking and freestyling, and it's something I say when I'm trying to identify a pattern for someone else. In some songs, phrases like that work when I'm trying to keep it conversational; but in a song like 'Pisces', which is meant to be more conceptual than casual, it would just muddy the waters. When you're working with concepts, it's like you're trying to refine ore into twenty-four-carat gold – you don't want any impurities in there! So maybe you record one version of the track that has all your little verbal tics in there. Then you can listen and edit out anything that isn't 100 per cent necessary. That's why 'Pisces' is a bit more of a challenging listen: I've taken away the scaffolding that would help you keep your grip on the song.

Elsewhere, though, those phrases are a way of pointing out inconsistencies and accidental jokes, the kinds of things in life that an artist should be alert to.

So in '33 Style', I say: 'It's funny how you'll take a life before you take your son to school'. I say it like that because I want to make an observation in a pointed way to an imagined listener. (In poetry, this is known as *apostrophe*.) But I want to take a step back from completely condemning my imagined listener. I'm not here to look down on anyone, I'm just here to notice patterns. Because if I said 'it's awful' or 'it's dreadful', I'm setting myself up as Mr Right. That's not the role of a writer.

If you set yourself up as judge, jury and executioner in a song, you won't actually encourage anyone to change. People won't feel they can connect with you. I play football a lot; I don't set myself up as the captain, but the team will tell me that's what they want. One time I asked them why, and they said that if someone misses a penalty, I'll tell him that he fucked up – but in a way that'll make him score the next one. There're two ways of conveying the exact same point. One is to say, 'Mate, you know you can put that away next time.' The other is to say, 'For fuck's sake, man, that was shit!' The difference is when you choose the second one, you've got one less player feeling like he can take a penalty next time.

People fuck up penalties when they overthink it. You'll see someone like Pogba run up like a duckling, getting caught up in the gimmick of the slow run, and then just shoot the ball off the crossbar. And you watch it thinking that if he'd just trusted his instincts, he'd have put it away. It's the responsibility of the rest of the team to make you feel comfortable enough to trust your instincts, rather than make you feel like you should never have stepped onto the pitch in the first place. And that's what the phrase 'it's funny how' does when I use it in a song. It makes the listener feel like I'm telling them something they already knew in the first place. Like they've got a moral compass telling them right from wrong, they just need to listen to it. The single most brutal thing you can ever say to a person is that they're not capable of being any better than they are.

You have to remember that when someone is listening to your music, you're in a position of power. They're looking up to you as the person with the fame, the skills, the money. I'm not saying that's right, but it's how society sets up the relationship between artist and audience. And because of this, it doesn't sit with me morally to say, 'I'm better than you.' If I was listening to someone judging me from up on a pedestal, I'd be angry – like, they've never known my struggle, so how can they denounce my flaws?

Instead, what I'm about is saying that we're all easy, we're all at different stages in life, but I feel you can do better – and you know you can too. Because as a man, and as a rapper, I benefited from people taking that time with me. As a rapper, you're taking on the role of the teacher, except there's no detention and no discipline – the only tool you have is your own personal experience, and making people feel they can relate to things you've been through. That's why you can't just jump from being a pupil to a teacher – you've got to live a life, and make some mistakes, first.

The lessons I learned from *Teacher's Training Day* to *Wretchrospective* were getting to know myself as a writer, what I can do that nobody else can, and how that matches up with the desires of my audience. There's a constant back-and-forth between the creative risks you need to take for yourself, and what your listeners need to help them enjoy what you're putting out there. There's a country singer who says that the trick to being an artist is to find out who you are, and do it on purpose. I'd say that's the first lesson. The second is to test your knowledge of yourself, and your craft, by taking it outside of a controlled environment. Animals can't grow bigger than the cage they're kept in. I mean, great white sharks don't survive in aquariums. That's why you need to get out of the classroom, and onto the battlefield.

2.

THE SOLDIER
('ANTWI')

> Then a soldier,
> Full of strange oaths and bearded like the pard,
> Jealous in honour, sudden and quick in quarrel,
> Seeking the bubble reputation
> Even in the cannon's mouth.

Antwi

I'm going through a break-up again
I see a dozen women and I break up with ten
I put 'em back together then I break 'em again
That's a match made in heaven or the thin line between
Love and hate that we cross till it makes us repent
I'm tryna let you know that this plays on my head
So you don't have to wait till I'm dead
Cause patience ain't one of your strengths
I waited a lifetime just to end up in the limelight
I write rhymes so they won't consider me an Einstein
While they was nominated for a Grammy for the ninth time
I was shedding tears with my family in a nine night
Nine time's over, I see man acting like Scarface
But they won't survive like Sosa
The night I woke up was when that black car rolled up

I was like nine years old, blud

Shopping for my mother, went to buy a tin of corned beef

Car lights flashing, is this when me and the Lord meet?

Tints rolled down, he shook his head when he saw me

I guess it wasn't for me

I've skipped death more than you've skipped breath

In your gym sesh, cardio won't make the kid Wretch

I've seen the prince cry when the king left

Is the queen gonna check mates or keep him in check?

Now I've seen a gunner ball rolling like him with Cech

Screaming 'suck ya mudda', incest

It makes you wonder where the kid went

When gunshot lick all ah him friend?

But fear won't allow you to be yourself

I'm Cool J in a Kangol, yeah, I did it well

Don't wanna see us bond, guess they'd rather us Stringer Bell

So that's why I punch above my weight till I beat Adele

I am Shakespeare with great hair

I'll probably be the next Wayne Hector in eight years

Tinchy had to break a few records to break here

Drake had to really take the pressure to take care

Take care of you, take care of me, take care of us

Take care of Mum, take care of everyone

You see how fast the hate turns to love

When everybody has to rate what you've done

Man will throw shade on the slums

But I rate what it made me become

See, I could have been wasted and dumb
Stuck with about an eighth in my lungs
Yeah, I pray the fuckboys keep their distance
I'm listening to Beres, putting up a resistance
You can keep your merits, man, I come for distinctions
I'm from the type of home where my brother's my sister
But that don't make a difference cuh I love her to bits and
We're just some have-nots tryna master the system
I had a mega drive when I was running the infants
Young Fire, Old Flame, you'll get bun in the distance
Wait for me
Mummy, won't you pray for me?
Heavy like I'm carrying a slave on me
But I'm just carrying the game on me
It's just a game
They say it's just a game, they say it's just a game
Well, if this is just a game
Why we dying just to play?
It's just a game
They said it's just a game, they say it's just a game
Well, if this is just a game
Why we dying just to play?
And for you, this might be just another eight
But for me, this is just another day
Just another race, in a race with the racists
Tryna make it off the slave ship
Can I get a break? Cause I don't want another chase

Cause I'm tired and there's no one to relay
Nor can nobody relate
My grandmother was a great
I had to put her in a grave, now my shoulder still aches
I had to carry her away
I'm still carrying the pain
Fuck marrying the fame
This is for my family to gain
And the young me's carrying my name

Pray for me, yeah
Pray for me, yeah
Pray for me, yeah

As an artist, you need the rain more than you need the sun. That's probably why some of the greatest poetry the world has ever seen came from the trenches – when you're surrounded by horror and death, your sanity depends on being able to find a way to process it. You might be fighting to survive, but you're writing so you can live. People forget that rap came from war: black GIs came back from the Vietnam War and would just rap about their experiences. It was a way to get the madness and the violence outside of themselves, put it into a shape and a form so they could make sense of it. And now when you look at the body count from knives and guns – on both sides of the Atlantic – it shouldn't be a surprise to anyone that rap is how young men make sense of the war that takes place on the streets. You don't need a uniform to be a soldier.

We grew up in a very, very tough environment. I was always taught that men don't cry. You fall over, you pick yourself up and you carry on. You don't cry. It's difficult, because inside I'm actually a mad emotional person.

I had to learn that men can shed tears. I can remember the first time I saw my dad and my uncles cry – it had a very strong effect on me. My granddad had just passed away, and my dad came round to my mum's; he spoke to her in the kitchen, and then they told us, and I was crying.

The funeral was a week or so later. My dad and my uncles are proper tough, old-school Tottenham men, and I remember looking over and seeing them all crying. And thinking, 'Rah! You can cry.' It was such a powerful thing. I was thirteen, fourteen at the time. I was looking to them for acceptance, to be allowed to cry. All the OGs from Tottenham are there and everyone's got a tear. It's allowed. It's cool.

At my grandma's funeral, I noticed my younger brothers and sisters looking at me in the same way, being surprised by the way I was behaving. It was Granny – it was a big thing for me. It was a tragedy. I was crying as I was carrying the coffin into the church. I was crying at home. I couldn't help it.

With 'Antwi', I'm talking about having to be tough and aware of your own pain at the same time. Originally, this song was just called 'Intro'. If you know a song is going to open your album, it has to be a statement of intent. It has to be powerful. It has to let people know what kind of mental landscape you've been living in. You have to reel in your audience with your tone, the track and what you're saying.

It's very rare that the first song you'll hear on an album is the first song that was written for that album. Making an LP is like mining for precious metals: first you dig up the ore, then you're extracting the gold from all the dirt. Then you go back and repeat that process dozens of times. It's only once you've done all that work, and you've beaten the gold into the shape of the necklace or whatever you're trying to make, that you can choose the gemstone that's going to catch your eye first.

When I wrote 'Antwi', I had already done the Fire in the Booth that was loud. The success of that freestyle had put it in my head as the model for the type of song I wanted to make. I wanted to recreate that intensity in a different way, and get it on my album. That 'Fire in the Booth pt 4' didn't flinch away from the darkness – it opened with 'Lately death's been getting ever so close / Been feeling spirits while I'm driving, I should get me a ghost'. So I knew with this one I had to dig in and find something brave again.

It was the beat that took me there first – there was something cinematic about it which just grabbed at my ear. Opening an album with this track feels like a film starting with a death. You're plunged into that moment of turmoil, and as a viewer you're knocked off your feet. The scene has grabbed you, and now the film's gonna hold you.

> *I'm going through a break-up again*
> *I see a dozen women and I break up with ten*
> *I put 'em back together then I break 'em again . . .*

This is putting you right in my state of mind. I hadn't actually gone through a romantic break-up; it was more that a relationship with someone I'd let get as close to me as it's possible to be had disintegrated. But those first lines of an album have to be a summary of where you are emotionally. You're not reporting word for word what's happened, you're finding the purest distillation of what you're feeling.

In 'Antwi', it's all about chaos and vulnerability. There's something kind of punk in starting in a moment of pure destruction. It's meant to be a hard listen – like hearing the horn of a lorry just before it runs you over, or like one of Hans Zimmer's film scores. In a way, I was channelling a bit of *The Dark Knight* on this song. Not Batman, but Heath Ledger's Joker. His performance was just so daring; he was acting from the very marrow of his bones.

You can't remember what Batman did in that film, but you can remember the Joker combing his hair with a knife. There's something about being an anti-hero that I find so much more interesting than a straightforward good guy. I wanted 'Antwi' to sound like the part of a film where a villain is explaining why he is the way he is. When I'm spitting about seeing a dozen women, breaking their hearts and breaking them again, I'm establishing my character as the guy who'll give you goosebumps the way a Fire in the Booth would. It's a venomous sentiment. I sound like a maniac – but I know I've made a good song because the listener can sympathise enough to follow me to the next line.

That's a match made in heaven or the thin line between
Love and hate that we cross till it makes us repent
I'm tryna let you know that this plays on my head
So you don't have to wait till I'm dead
Cause patience ain't one of your strengths

This is the point where I'm trying to address the person who's driven me to this moment. Here the language I use shifts up a gear into a much more religious and morbid tone. It raises the emotional stakes of the verse. It's life and death; it's sin and forgiveness. I'm taking you to the church and to my coffin via both sides of the afterlife! What I'm saying is that our relationship has got so toxic that it's only when I'm gone that they'll be able to understand they were on my mind the whole time I was alive – but instead of having to wait, I'm just going to set it out now. In a weird way, I'm being nice! I just had to be ruthless first to get there.

They say the Devil has all the best tunes. I don't think it's that simple, though. A world-class writer doesn't just make violence or cruelty sound appealing; they make violence and cruelty sound plausible because they've shown you all the steps and reasoning leading up to it. Any rapper can talk about selling drugs, or beefing, or whatever. But that's just gonna fall flat if you can't tell me why it is you made those decisions. Don't just tell me about shotting; tell me what your mum is like, how you were born into this life. Tell me what you've seen. As a listener, I want to learn about your highest highs and your lowest lows. You can't depict chaos without showing me your reasoning.

Spitting aggressively isn't itself a bad thing. If it wasn't for that style we wouldn't have had Dizzee Rascal, Lethal B or Ghetts. Like when I was younger, I was just writing about shotting. But I realised people could be understanding of even the most extreme situations if you just take some time to explain how you got there. There's a song called 'Have Mercy' where I'm talking about all those things which you'd think are unforgivable. And I wrote that song at the same time as I was living that life – even as I was doing those things, I felt a strong sense of remorse. I knew that feeling had to make its way into the music.

I didn't have to be vulnerable in 'Antwi'. I could've said those first eight lines in just two words: 'Fuck bitches.' But then you'd have just glazed over, because you've heard that song before. And if you're not attentively listening to the song, then you're not understanding me as a person. The only time this should be the case is when I deliberately want to leave you in limbo.

That's what all this stuff in the newspapers gets wrong about drill. From the outside listening in, lots of people look at drill artists and just see an animal. But even an animal has a heart. It's a very young genre – not only in terms of how long it's been around, but the age of the MCs as well. These are young guys with talent and a voice, but they're in a place of pain – and no one's there to mentor them. Lots of these drill artists have only just turned sixteen, and I think there's just a lack of life experience there, which means you don't get the insight alongside the narrative of the violence that's happening. At that age, I don't know how accountable someone can be for the version they give. Could Heath Ledger have played the Joker when he was a teenage actor? Probably not. You need time for your body to grow into the skin you've been given, and it's the same with writing.

I think these drill MCs just need lyricists who are already up there in the elite to show them how to elevate their work to the next level. It's not about changing the sound, or making drill less aggressive. It's about making music that shows an understanding of *why* the aggression is there in the first place. It doesn't have to be the case that you write a whole new song. Just a line. You can tell me, 'I came home, smashed up my house. I smashed someone's car window. I've run into a shop and smashed it to pieces', but it's gonna get repetitive unless at some point you tell me *why* you've done all that. You might have heard that your brother's been locked up, or your dad's got cancer. Tell me something which puts the destruction into context. Otherwise the whole thing just sounds erratic.

That doesn't mean you have to say 'sorry'. In 'Antwi', awareness is more important than an apology. It's more about touching on that feeling of wanting to repent, even if forgiveness is just out of reach. That's why I go back to the moment when I lost my innocence as a child:

> *The night I woke up was when that black car rolled up*
> *I was like nine years old, blud*
> *Shopping for my mother, went to buy a tin of corned beef*

56

Car lights flashing, is this when me and the Lord meet?
Tints rolled down, he shook his head when he saw me
I guess it wasn't for me

When I was growing up, the beef in and around Tottenham was at its pinnacle. One night, some of the other side came round my estate looking for a boy who lived behind me. The boy they were looking for was way older than me – but it was a dark night, and I was a tall kid. I left my house to see a Ford Fiesta XR2i careen around the corner with its window rolled down. And even though I was just nine years old, I knew exactly what that meant.

If the man on the trigger had just been a touch quicker off the mark, I would have died that night. But by some miracle he took a moment to look into my face and see that I was a child. That's when I realised that it didn't matter whether I was involved in that war or not: it might come knocking on my door (or pulling up outside my house) anyway. It was the first time I thought it might be safer to just actively make the choice to get involved, and that way I could protect myself. You could rely on people ringing you up to warn you when the other side was about: 'It's gonna be one of those nights, make sure you're in.' After a while, the back-and-forth and all the madness just became normal.

It's even worse today. When I was growing up, you at least had to travel to a different postcode, but now it's neighbours fighting home and away. North London is tearing itself apart. Young people are going to the funerals of their friends before they're going to the funerals of their grandparents. It's a war out there for them – and they're coming back like soldiers who've lost fifteen or twenty men. They're traumatised. The other day, I got sent a video of a boy who'd been stabbed in the leg. It was terrible. Here's this kid who's bleeding on the floor, screaming and afraid. I know him personally – he's never done anything to anyone, he was just in the wrong place at the wrong time. Some boys from the other side were out looking for someone else and they found him instead. The worst part is that when this boy's mum was told what had happened to her son, she had a stroke. Thank God she pulled through. But imagine living your life legitimately, doing everything right, but something like that still happens to you. Where do you go after this? You get stitched up in the hospital but what about the scars you can't see? You have to come home to a place where you nearly died without anyone to look after you. If you're a black boy from a certain area, innocence is a luxury you don't get to enjoy for very long.

Not everyone gets to age the same way. I'm thirty-three, and I've gone to more funerals than I've had years on this earth. Feeling the weight of a coffin on your shoulder forces you to grow up. When I say in 'Antwi' that 'I waited a lifetime just to end up in the limelight', I'm not only talking about how waiting for success felt like an eternity; I'm telling you my years have been measured by the number of lives I've seen lost in that time. I've seen too many graves dug too young. And lots of those deaths could have been me: 'I've skipped death more than you've skipped breath / In your gym sesh, cardio won't make the kid Wretch'. When you're so close to death for so much of your life, you start to realise you couldn't make the music that you do without it. And you can't fake that perspective – you can't work those artistic muscles in a controlled environment like a gym. You've got to be out on the real battlefield to become a soldier. Even if you don't use these emotions in your art right away, keep them in storage. One day you'll find something that evokes that feeling, and you'll be able to put it into words.

In this life, you can only fight fire with fire in certain situations. I like to think of myself as being so rational. But if I see something that's plainly wrong that I can't explain, I have irrational thoughts. I act irrationally. It's a lack of control. It's knowing I won't be able to control myself. I'll be the idiot trying to turn cars over at a protest. A philosopher said that the thing that separates the government from the rest of us is they're the only ones allowed to use force. So it's not a moral difference: it's just a monopoly on violence. They will come down like a ton of bricks if you ever try to disrupt that. Whenever you fight, you can't go further than the wrong that's been done to you in the first place. And you'd better prepare yourself for the consequences. What's the first thing you learn as a soldier? Stick to your guns, or don't show your guns at all.

There are some paving stones on the ground that you can't just step around. You have to walk over them in order to get to where you're meant to go. When you grow up in that kind of environment, you have a decision to make. Is violence going to affect your life, is it going to become your life, or is it going to take your life? For a while I let it become my life, because I didn't think there was an option of things being different for me. But it got to a point where I knew it was going to be music or nothing.

As people around me started doing serious time inside, I began to see the reality of the situation I was in. Someone got two years, then another got five. Someone else got eight. The government spent something like £400,000 on assigned police to my estate – and one day they did a swoop, where several houses at once got raided. I'm talking about battering rams, floodlights on the balcony – it was like a siege.

A lot of people I knew got arrested. The rest of us were in shock afterwards, like we were trying to shake off a hit with a stun gun. Numb, we were counting off who'd been snatched up. But then a guy called Baff came up to us – he was Chip's manager – and asked why we were all standing around looking surprised. His own mum's house had had its door kicked in, and his brother had been taken. And yet he told us off for being naive: 'How has this come as a shock to you? This is what happens.' Baff didn't spare me one bit: 'Wretch, you're the best rapper in Tottenham. We shouldn't even be seeing you, because you should be in the studio every hour of the day. But you're out here playing a game that you're eventually going to lose.' And he was right. Why put yourself in a game of cat and mouse? There's no such thing as escape. Even when Jerry would get away one episode, he'd get dragged back to do the same thing again in the next one. You're always gonna get caught – if not this time, then the next time some cat out there wants a snack.

What Baff told me that day changed my whole life. It was one of those moments when you catch a glimpse of the path ahead if you don't make a significant change to what you're doing. I knew if I didn't act on what he'd said, there'd come a day when his words would haunt me; Baff's voice would be ringing in my ears as I paced around a prison cell. I suppose I could make that decision because I never felt passionate about dealing. Some guys want to get to the top of the food chain, but all I ever wanted was enough. All I would take to sell was what I could pay for immediately. I was working in Sainsbury's at the time, so I knew my rent was cool; I just needed that extra two grand to pay for studio time and record the eight songs I'd been working on. Why would I want four grand when that would take time away from what I actually wanted to do? But then it makes you question why you're taking that risk in the first place. Why am I taking that break from the studio to go out and top up? If you're not going to be Pablo Escobar or anyone like that, the next thing that happens after getting a little bit of money is you're gonna sit down for two years inside and you're gonna waste time. The time comes when you decide you're going to spend two and a half years trying to make this work, or you're going to spend the best of your youth staring at a wall. So after that raid on the estate, me and Zeon decided to take the money we'd made and put it all into making music. He's still my manager to this day.

It's because of where we come from that Baff was able to build up the Alwayz Recording brand the way he did. I mean, one hand washes the other, so we all played our part in it, but we were using Baff's sink, so to speak. Growing up hungry means you've got a different stomach. It means you take a bite at the apple, looking to take the whole hand with you.

Even when you leave that life behind, an artist has to stay with the pain. That's why the next bit of that eight in 'Antwi' goes:

> I've seen the prince cry when the king left
> Is the queen gonna check mates or keep him in check?
> Now I've seen a gunner ball rolling like him with Cech
> Screaming 'suck ya mudda', incest
> It makes you wonder where the kid went
> When gunshot lick all ah him friend?

It's hard being a prince without a father to guide you. I've seen generations of lost boys after their dads have gone – killed, locked up or walked away – and their mums at a loss for what to do. Does the queen try to rebuild her life after the king has left? How long are you a widow before you can become a woman again? There are no simple answers to these questions. It's hard being a mother to a son, much harder than it is to be a father. Nine times out of ten, it's her that's got to be around 24/7. A man always has the option of leaving, and then suddenly a woman has to be both the mum and the dad. It's so rare to see it the other way around that Rio Ferdinand gets a whole documentary about raising kids on his own (even though he's a hero in my eyes!). When's the last time you saw that for a single mother? And on top of every little practical thing she has to deal with, she can't take her eye off her boy for one second. Because if life takes a little left turn, her prince will become that gunner shooting someone down – or getting shot down himself.

You can write yourself into a corner when you muse on death for too long. Think about it: how many people have you known to talk their way out of a coffin? As a lyricist I know I need to create a break in that eight-bar. That's what 'Screaming "suck ya mudda", incest' is for. It's one of those lines that I know a crowd is going to sing back at me, so it functions as a kind of release after building up all that tension. If I'm writing about being born into a world where you have to fight as soon as you can leave the house, then I need the audience to feel that way too. It's a way of getting inside the skin of that kid who just wants to kick out at the world. This is the writer's privilege: you get to speak in someone else's voice without losing your own in the process, knowing that other people will relate to the character you've conjured up. When I was in my teens, I'd have been yelling that line at a show, probably without thinking about it too deeply. That's why I don't just want to give you the explosion: I have to leave you reflecting on the debris. What happens to the child soldier standing when all of his bredrins have been killed?

Bravery isn't simply about putting yourself in dangerous situations and fronting it out. It's about having the courage to stop fronting completely. When I say that 'fear won't allow you to be yourself', I'm talking about the prisons we live in that are of our own making. You can be in jail, or trapped in an environment that you grow up in, but worst of all is to live inside the invisible walls of other people's expectations. You have to make an active decision to go beyond just surviving, to living the way you want to live. That can mean a lot of different things. For me, it was about being forced to stand on my own two feet. When my mum found out that I was getting involved in wrong things, she knew she had a choice: she could try and force-feed me a lesson in morality, or she could compel me to figure it out on my own. Kicking me out of her house was the best thing she ever did for me. It sounds weird to say that, because at the time I was mad as hell, but there's a logic to it.

When I was under her wing, I never had to be excellent at anything. I had a natural gift for English, but I never got As or A*s because I didn't do my coursework. I enjoyed drama, but I didn't take the time to rehearse my lines properly – when I'd get to the end of the bit I could remember, I'd just start riffing. And with music, I just didn't try. I'd write the first two bars of an eight and go over them obsessively, until I lost patience and rushed the next six. I had to live without the safety net to stop fucking about on the tightrope, and start taking my craft seriously. It's like playing poker, but only being good at it when the stakes are high. I can never perform if I'm just playing for matchsticks – I'm betting the house! There's something about taking away the safety net which makes you a lot more serious about who you are and what you're doing. If my mum hadn't been brave enough to make me live alone, I might not have been brave enough to make music at all.

Some people resent having the burden of responsibility, but I couldn't have become the artist I am today without it. That's what the 'take care' section is referring to: 'Take care of you, take care of me, take care of us / Take care of Mum, take care of everyone'. In repeating 'take care' as a refrain, I'm conveying the sense of relentless pressure that I live under. Another artist might do the same thing in order to say that they just can't hack it any more, that they feel they might disintegrate at any moment. For them it's like being Buckaroo – if they have to shoulder one more burden, they're going to snap. But there's another way to look at it: it's the weight of the world that turns coal into diamonds. Precious gems aren't formed in the sunshine, so others might 'throw shade on the slums / But I rate what it made me become'. I'm grateful for the fact that I can take care of people now. It's the opposite of the whole 'Mo Money Mo Problems' mindset – if I'm in a position where I'm happy to give back to the place that made me, I'm not going to look at it as people trying to take what I've got. I don't want the kids who grow up on my estate to feel like they're so worthless that people will just abandon them the moment they make enough money to move elsewhere. I'll keep coming back to give back. I want them to have something to look up to. There's a difference between saying that where I grew up was hard, and saying that where I grew up has nothing of value. I can live anywhere, but Tottenham is the only place I'll call home.

You're always going to feel an affinity with the people who have experienced the same sort of struggles as you have, and for me as a lyricist, I need to represent that in my work. That's why in 'Antwi' I go on to say,

> You can keep your merits, man, I come for distinctions
> I'm from the type of home where my brother's my sister
> But that don't make a difference cuh I love her to bits and
> We're just some have-nots tryna master the system

What I'm talking about here is that me and my little sister have always been the renegades of the family.

She's like a Queen Latifah character: as soon as she could dress herself, she never wore a skirt again. She always looked up to me more than our other sisters: she walks like me, she thinks like me, she talks like me. When she walks around Tottenham, people will think she's my brother. She's had to fight other people's expectations of what a girl should be like in order to live her identity. That's a soldier right there. And we've never talked about it together. So I wanted to be able to put it down in a song for her, and for anyone else who might be struggling to be accepted for who they are. I like that the wording is a bit ambiguous: when I say 'my brother's my sister', you're forced to take a moment and mull over what I mean. It could be that my sister took a role of guiding me like a big brother would. Or that I have a brother who's very feminine and caring. I wanted people to be able to associate their own situation with what I'm saying, and draw some courage from it. Because we live in a very judgemental, very restrictive society. You're having to battle just to be able to live how you want to live. As a musician you should always aim to stand with people that society would otherwise seek to put in a box. We should all look at each other as accomplices in trying to tear down an unjust system.

My sister taking the risk of being her authentic self is one of the things which inspired me to be bold with my music. When I first started out on pirate radio, rapping at 140 bpm didn't quite sit right with me. I could spit fast, but what I was actually saying was going over people's heads. No one was hearing me. I found the traditional grime format very restrictive; if I stuck to it religiously, I could never have made a tune like 'Pisces' or 'Can't Say Sorry', or a song that girls would like. For me, starting to make the songs I wanted to was being fearless. The attitude on my estate was that you couldn't make songs at 90 bpm, or write about things that weren't shotting or whatever. But if you maintain that mentality, you'll only ever write songs that don't circulate outside of your immediate environment. Fear is keeping you boxed in on your block. But if my sister could find it within herself to walk down the street and not care about being judged, then I could make a 'Don't Go' or a '6 Words'. You can't live knowing that a part of you isn't being represented.

So far I've talked about 'Antwi' in terms of the conflicts you experience outside of yourself – on the street, or rebelling against society. But it'd be boring if the song never strayed from being about strength. It's not a compelling fight scene if there's never a risk of losing: in order to get you on my side as a listener, I have to make you feel the weight of what I'm carrying, and make you feel the fear that I might lose my footing. That's why the next section of the song – 'Wait for me' – is much more a stream of consciousness than what comes before. I'm not thinking about the rigid structure of eights or sixteens any more. What holds it together is the *assonance* (rhyming on a vowel sound). So here 'pray', 'slave', 'race', 'grave', 'aches', 'game', 'great', 'eight', 'day', 'play', 'fame' and 'gain' are all connected by that shared 'ay' sound. The song loses its internal structure, but in a controlled way so you know I'm doing it on purpose. It's important that writers utilise verbal tools to demonstrate their own awareness of what it is they're doing. Effects like assonance communicate the sense that you're deliberate in what you're doing. It helps establish a pattern for the listener to follow, and not get confused when you're depicting the experience of being lost.

The religious language of 'repent' from the start of the song makes a comeback with the refrain of 'pray for me'. I pointed out earlier that I never actually say 'sorry' in this song – which raises the question, what happens to someone who can never make amends? They're damned for eternity, but they're still yearning for some redemption. That's probably a sentiment shared by most people on this earth. In the absence of forgiveness, all you can do is demonstrate some understanding and hope that others respond with empathy.

For me, you can't understand your personal life if you don't know your people's history. And that knowledge is a burden as well as a blessing – 'Heavy like I'm carrying a slave on me'. Those are my ancestors that I'm feeling. Because the minute you become aware of what's happened to black people throughout history, you start asking yourself how high you can go with everything on your shoulders. If you're a lyricist and not just a writer, you can hint towards history without having to make it explicit. For instance, the refrain of 'pray for me', after the mentions of slavery, gets you thinking about the spirituals that slaves sang on the plantations, or gospel music from when people were fighting for their civil rights. If you're a black man trying to make it in this world, work isn't just a rat race. It's trying to stay one step ahead of the racists who want to keep you on the slave ship: incarcerated, in chains, or lost to the waves. It's a whole different level of drive when you don't have the option of ever putting a foot wrong.

Music as an industry has a high death toll. Think about just how many died before their time – Amy Winehouse, 2Pac, Billie Holiday, Mac Miller, Cadet. An artist needs to make music in order to survive, but the paradox is that the very same thing can be what kills you. Ask me why I care so much, and you may as well ask a drowning man why he's struggling for oxygen. For a listener it might 'be just another eight', but for me it's life and death all rolled into one. My whole family are relying on me, and I've got no one I can pass the baton to – 'there's no one to relate'. The only person who could understand that pressure was my grandmother, and now she's gone. Being the pall-bearer is a weight that will never leave me.

I might feel the weight of the greats on my shoulder, but I know I'm only where I am because I'm standing on the shoulders of giants. And one of those giants was Richard Antwi. Lots of you might have heard of him as a music lawyer, but he was so much more than that. He was a mentor, a powerhouse, a legend in his own right. It was him and Twin B who sat down with me and Zeon and brought us onto the Ministry of Sound record label, through a label of their own called LEVELS. Richard's vision wasn't just about the commercial side of music; I'd always send him material I was working on because I trusted his judgement. He was the soldier's soldier, a man with real honour and integrity. I'm not sure my career would have got to where it is today without him, and after I heard the news of his sudden passing, I couldn't think of a better way to thank him than giving the last ever song I sent to him his name. You've heard many intros in your life. But there's only one 'Antwi'.

3.

THE LOVER
('COOKED FOOD', 'HIS & HERS')

And then the lover,
Sighing like furnace, with a woeful ballad
Made to his mistress' eyebrow.

Cooked Food

Cause, oh girl, I love you like cooked food (cooked food)

Chick King, the best thigh and the breast
Everybody wants a piece on the ends
I paid for it, I won't even pretend
Thought our shit was sorted till she got grease on my bed
And I went quiet on her
Yeah, hit the silence on her
She was weighting me down, I had to diet on her
Yeah, she fucks with me cuh I'm getting chips
And I'll always have a wingman if she got relatives
No, baby, I'll let you know, baby
You're gonna kill me if I see you every day
Let me go, baby, uh, just let me go, baby
You know it's been a generation game

From my old lady, yeah, and her old lady
You're gonna feel me if I see you every day
In my postcode, and I won't say no, so
Why you acting like you don't know?

I love you like cooked food
Oh girl, I love you like cooked food
Even though I don't cook food, oh
You know I love you like cooked food

You should never dress like you're under-priced
Cause they ain't seeing where you're coming from in life
Standing on the market, everybody wants a slice
Think your mother dropped the egg for them to cut
    you with a knife?
It's a cutthroat business, I trust no women
I give the world my heart and hope the love grows in 'em
And one day we'll have our own son or chicken
They're both born gold and they cluck no different
No way, I love it when you dress saucy
And the way you make it dip when you're naughty
Are you really gonna keep me fit till I'm forty?
In casinos, tryna get chips to divorce me
All jokes aside, I'll get some fries with you
And I don't have a side chick because I side with you
Yeah, the weather's hot, I guess I'll fry with you
I'm tryna bubble like Coke and supersize the view

I love you like cooked food (oh girl, I love you like
    cooked food)
Oh girl, I love you like cooked food (you know I love
    you like cooked food)
Even though I don't cook food (even though I don't
    cook food)
You know I love you like cooked food (oh girl, I love you
    like cooked food)

Remember when I was hungry doing stick-ups on
    the ends?
You're the only one that kept me fed
I got my Ps up so I had to let 'em spread
Now everywhere I go, I'm dropping bread on chicken
    heads
I'm happy that I now see you all over the ends
Cause I can see the power in them legs
Think I can get some salad with them breasts?
If you can still fly, I'll stay with you till the end

I love you like cooked food
Oh girl, I love you like cooked food
Even though I don't cook food
Oh girl, I love you like cooked food

Verse, whether it's rap or poetry, is a special kind of art. It announces to you, straight up, that in order to find a deeper truth, you can't trust what you're reading and what you're hearing. Writing a verse is professional deception. The simplest phrase can have dozens of different meanings – a slight change in pronunciation, or a word with more than one definition, and suddenly a whole new universe of interpretation is unlocked. Verse wants to frustrate you. It wants to make you obsess over each syllable or silence. It dares you to take it at face value, then turns your world upside down with a single line. You believe in the writer, and yet you can't trust them. And I suppose that's why it's so perfect for writing about love: both romance and rhyming invite misunderstanding.

And that's part of the joy, right? Because if everyone

only said exactly what they meant, there'd be no such thing as flirting. Imagine life without double entendre and innuendo, half-jokes and risqué implications. It would make things so boring. You might as well couple up by committee. But that same potential for misinterpretation is what turns relationships toxic. One person grasps the wrong end of the stick, and then next thing you know the whole forest gets chopped down. The two songs I'm comparing here – 'Cooked Food' and 'His & Hers' – both play on the idea of people not saying what they mean. But the emotional outcomes are very, very different.

It's funny that I'm so interested in the theme of miscommunication in my songs, because in my own love life I really prioritise being direct. I was never particularly nervous around girls. I had no expectations, so for me there was nothing to be frightened of. I could talk to girls anywhere. It's either a yes or a no. It's black and white. And maybe that's something girls liked, the fact that I could just walk over and start talking. I wasn't trying to be cool, I was being friendly. It was always a good energy, a good vibe. And I think people respond well to that.

My first crush began in primary school. Just a little 'I'll hold your bag' thing. And even though we were only kids, there was a lot of love there. But she had a baby when she was very young, and left school when she was in Year 9. I still see her around today, and message her now and again to see how she's doing. You never forget your first love. It sets the tone for everything that comes after. Nostalgia, how memory works to create a longing for the past, is one of the most potent forces in love. Think about how a certain fragrance can remind you of a former flame. The scent of a perfume can take you back to all those good times you had, and you remember a summer night when you stayed up till sunrise talking rather than the time you got an ashtray chucked at your head. Nostalgia isn't always honest, but it's powerful.

I'm tapping into a sense of affection and nostalgia in 'Cooked Food'. It's set up from the get-go as a love song: there's a gentle piano intro, a crooning vocal singing, 'Cause, oh girl, I love you like cooked food'. I'd like to take the credit for the simile, but 'I love you like cooked food' is a very common Jamaican saying. It's always resonated with me: in a phrase so simple, you've got this very rich idea of love being something that's nourishing, that makes you feel warm inside, that you need to survive. And the reference to Chick King (the greatest chicken shop in the northern hemisphere – don't @ me) in the opening line of the first verse puts you right back in that spot of being young and just roaming around the ends with your girl. You're not going to the Savoy Grill, you're going to your local chicken shop!

With the hook leading into the verse, the immediate impression you get is that I'm writing a song comparing a girl who I've been with for a long time to fried chicken. It's playful and a bit mischievous. In poetry, *blazon* is the technique of comparing a woman's body to a set of objects – like jewels or constellations, or maybe a feast. Your hair is like the Milky Way, your eyes are like the stars, blah blah blah. It became such a cliché to write a poem talking about a lover in this way that even Shakespeare had to take the piss a bit. He wrote a sonnet saying 'My mistress' eyes are *nothing* like the sun'; it then goes on to list all the beautiful things that she doesn't resemble. It's a bit of a par on whoever he's writing about, really.

So, on first listening, you think I'm doing something similar here – drawing comparisons between a woman and a chicken. But even though I'm celebrating her ('the best thigh and the breast'), it's not quite complimentary. Of all the foods you'd like to be compared to – dark chocolate, intoxicating wine, ripe fruit – chicken isn't exactly the most sexy or sensual. And that's before you get to the fact that I don't even eat chicken any more! If I'm talking about a woman in this way, it's dehumanising. I'm even saying that 'I paid for it, I won't even pretend', as though I'm talking about a relationship with an escort: I 'had to diet on her' when she became too demanding ('She was weighting me down'). If you take 'Cooked

Food' on a surface level, it's a love song telling a girl: 'I'm saying you might just be a piece of meat, but you're a very tasty one.'

But read the lyrics a little closer. I'm not *actually* comparing a woman to a chicken: I'm comparing a chicken to a woman. It's a subtle difference which results in a wildly different meaning! Instead of using figurative language to dehumanise a woman, I'm using it to anthropomorphise my (former) favourite food! So all the stuff that looks like a metaphor on first glance – 'Thought our shit was sorted till she got grease on my bed', 'Everybody wants a piece on the ends' – is actually just literal. Chicken grease made a mess of my sheets. Everyone I know wants to grab a piece of the best meal deal in town. I'm not talking about ending a relationship with a girl, I'm talking about gaining too much weight from eating chicken every day. If a metaphor is a bluff – 'You think I'm talking about this, but I'm talking about *that*' – this song is a double-bluff blazon: 'You don't believe I'm talking about this, but I am.' In 'Cooked Food', there are two stories running parallel. One is about a turbulent love affair, where you can't get enough even though it's destroying you – the growing awareness that you need to move on and mature from the very thing you used to rely on to survive. And the other's about having a girlfriend.

If it's a love song, then 'Cooked Food' is about my

love of wordplay. Like the whole way through, I'm playing with you. It's never 100 per cent clear who or what I'm talking to. This use of 'you' is another example of apostrophe in verse, and here I'm deliberately blurring the object of my thoughts. There's just so much language that straddles both sides of food and flirting – like 'I love it when you dress saucy / And the way you make it dip when you're naughty'. Obviously women (and some men) dress saucy, and that's a part of being attracted to someone. But you also 'dress' a plate, and a naughty dip might be a pot of hot sauce. It's kind of funny to think there'll be people listening to this song and really feeling themselves, when I'm actually addressing a chicken.

I told you never to trust a writer!

Even though I'm playing tricks on you in 'Cooked Food', there are still serious things I'm trying to get across. You can't rely on straight banter – there has to be depth to it. I wanted it to have meaning. That's the thing that really took Childish Gambino to the next level. In his early work, he rapped the same way he did stand-up comedy: set-up, punchline, set-up, punchline . . . And it was good, but was it great? But then after *Awaken, My Love!* he showed a real sense of perspective. His work was more risk-taking and experimental; he started being serious with his social commentary. And he moved from being a sick spitter to a true artist. So, as well as talking about the health issues that come with fast food every day, I'm also genuinely exploring the way food shapes our society.

They say the way to a man's heart is through his stomach, and I suppose it's one of those things that became a cliché because it's true. Food talks when words fail. Whenever you're struggling, you'll know your real friends by the ones who make sure you're eating. Food can say 'I love you', 'I'm worried about you', or 'Hey, remember this?' A dish isn't just made of ingredients, it's made of memories. I'm definitely not the first to say this! The French writer Marcel Proust wrote about how tasting a madeleine dipped in tea could transport him back to his childhood. Something as simple as that tiny cake took him back to Sunday mornings with his favourite aunt, where she would share a madeleine with him before they went to church. And along with love, the taste would remind him of loss. The dessert, for Proust, was bittersweet.

I considered calling this song 'Soul Food' because, beyond all the wordplay, the thing holding this track together is sincerity. I'm rapping about something I feel very deeply. The song came from listening to the melody first, and thinking that it sounded very warm. And that's what took me back to thinking about the role food had played in my upbringing. The food that will take you back will differ depending on your background. For a French author, it was a fancy cake. For someone else it might be biriyani, or bagels, or banana cake. And for people from my community, it's chicken. You can't write a song like this without having an understanding of chicken shop culture.

My starting point is affection. Because for us growing up, chicken shops were social institutions. If your mum was a single parent working long hours, that was a reliable and cheap way for you to get fed. Chick King was right next to my school, so from Year 7 I could get chicken and chips for 90p. Knowing them for so long, they began to feel like family in Tottenham. When I was shotting and the streets could feel like a hostile place, Chick King was always a place of sanctuary. And thinking about chicken more broadly, when it was Mum's payday on Friday, we'd go to KFC to get a Bargain Bucket as a treat. For us, that was like whoo! Backflips in the house, roly-polies all over the place.

We'd also have Sunday dinner, which was so much more than just a meal. It was a ritual: Grandma going to the meat market and bringing back the chicken for my mum to skin and season. That's what I'm talking about when I say, 'You know it's been a generation game / From my old lady, yeah, and her old lady'. The chicken would be at the centre of the kitchen, all the women of my family orbiting it like the solar system – cooking, chatting, listening to music. I learned so much there, and that's why talking about chicken in this way feels embedded in me. There's that annoying stereotype about black people and chicken, but what I'm doing here is flipping it and turning a thing that's used against us into a source (or sauce) of strength. It shouldn't be something that's mocked. It's culture. Recipes passed down from parent to child are what nourishes your family tree. A beloved cookbook tells you as much about your heritage as a genealogy. So, in that way, 'Cooked Food' is a sincere celebration of women through chicken – it's just not the one I tricked you into thinking it was.

It's important to have a variety of tones in a song that's warm – because without the contrast, you won't feel the sentiment. If I set out to write something sunny and breezy, I want to see if it'll survive the odd drizzle of rain. So as well as 'Cooked Food' having that genuine theme of celebrating women, I also explore the idea of how women are dehumanised through being seen as pieces of meat. Because of the slipperiness in my use of apostrophe, I change towards addressing a woman in the second verse without ever making it feel like a shift in gears.

The reference to 'Standing on the market, everybody wants a slice' is a criticism of the way female bodies are commodified. That's not just in advertising and the media – women who aren't even in the public eye have to shoulder massive expectations in how they're meant to look. And even if they live up to those expectations, they get demonised for it! I had in my head the idea of a meat market where all the butchers are out on the street hawking their wares. And then there's a woman walking down the middle of the road, and all those yells and shouts turn into catcalling her. If a woman looks good, and men find her attractive, she gets punished for it. And if she's considered unattractive, she has to go through a whole different thing: she starts doubting the body and bone structure that her parents gave her, and starts wondering if a surgeon could do a better job. That's the point I'm making when I say, 'Think your mother dropped the egg for them to cut you with the knife?' Here, I'm talking about the extreme measures some people take to change how they look. Girls are putting all sorts of shit into themselves just to measure up to a standard of beauty that's gonna change in ten years anyway. Cosmetic surgery is literally 'a cutthroat business'; but then again, so is romance.

It's on this thought that the verse takes a little turn. I'm the kind of writer who likes to set themselves a challenge when they write: if I set out to write on a particular sentiment, I like to see how far I can stray without losing the thread entirely. So with a song like

'Cooked Food', the vibe is very upbeat. You're meant to feel a glow from the inside out. The challenge then is to introduce a moment that isn't just a focus on the more serious things in life, but goes against the grain: 'It's a cutthroat business, I trust no women'. That's a strange phrase to hear in a love song. But it's the culmination of that train of thought about how men and women are brought up to relate to one another, and how the pressures put on women actually break down the trust that relationships need in order to work.

The skilful bit comes when you yank the song back into the sentiment that it originated in, so that dark thought is fleeting but not disposable. The point of love is that you fall for someone against your better judgement, that even though you've learned the hard way not to trust, the lesson never sticks. So I go from that statement about emotionally withdrawing and follow it up with the complete opposite: 'I give the world my heart and hope the love grows in 'em'. Because that's what you do when you publish your work – you're putting your heart in the hands of every person who picks up your record.

Being emotionally vulnerable in this way allows me to follow that positive thread again and come back to the relationship theme: 'And one day we'll have our own son or chicken / They're both born gold and they cluck no different'. I mean, come on, is there anything cuter than thinking about how babies and newly hatched chicks are similar? It's meant to make you feel tender, to soften into thinking about a future spent with someone you love. Choosing to commit to someone starts with something very simple – a gesture, a shared meal. 'All jokes aside, I'll get some fries with you': that means we're getting serious, we're embarking on a journey together. Although, even though I said I'm not kidding, it doesn't mean I can't make jokes ('And I don't have a side chick because I side with you'). Devotion shouldn't be boring!

In the last verse, I try and connect all these things. First, there's my memory of the chicken shop feeding me when nothing else could ('Remember when I was hungry doing stick-ups on the ends? / You're the only one that kept me fed'), and then I link together my own personal success and being able to spend money on girls ('I got my Ps up so I had to let 'em spread / Now everywhere I go, I'm dropping bread on chicken heads') to the growth of the local chicken shop all over the city ('I'm happy that I now see you all over the ends'). I even structure the bars a bit differently here, and use my delivery to make it more punchy than conversational, to really hammer the point home. So when I get to ''Cause I can see the power in them legs', I'm talking about *everything*: 'them legs' are what powers the yutes in the ends, it's the glue that holds our social fabric together, and it also refers to the body of the woman in the blazon. You're supposed to feel breathless, like this verse is pulsing with all the meanings layered into it.

This song comes from a good place. Chicken shops get a lot of stick for being cheap or shabby. But I wanted to write something that could set the story straight. It's like everyone's been dissing my little cousin, and I'm trying to introduce you to him properly. I'm bringing you over and saying that he's got his flaws here and there but this is what I love about him. It's about showing what kind of investment socially marginalised people have in the things that are normally looked down upon. In 'Cooked Food', chicken isn't just a metaphor for one specific thing, it's what's called a *floating signifier* – something you can project a lot of other meanings onto, like family, friendship, love and culture. A straightforward love song couldn't convey all of that. My version of a love song, this *bluff blazon*, is unfaithful to the idea of one person, but it's loyal to the variety and vibrancy I see in the ends.

Interlude: A Marriage Made in Heaven

Like I said earlier, 'Cooked Food' came about from just listening to the track and letting the sound guide the sentiment. Being a rapper requires being deliberate with your words, sure, but you also have to learn how to let go of control – to let something flow through you, and take you where it wants to go. If you come with too many preconceived ideas when you listen to a track, all you'll hear is the crunching of gears. You can't force a word to work when the music is saying no. And unless you're making your own track, rapping over a beat involves being a vehicle for someone else's art as much as they are a vessel for yours.

Producers often say I'm the kind of artist who knows what he wants. When it comes to choosing beats, I let myself be moved by my gut. What am I vibing with? What conjures up strong emotion? What sets off a chain reaction in my mind? Afterwards, I think a bit more strategically about what could fit a gap on the record. But that first moment of emotional connection is really important: without it, there's simply not enough inspiration to keep me fired up and engaged throughout a studio session. But I've worked out over time that the producers who I enjoy collaborating with the best know what I want even before I do! They'll sit me down and play a few tracks, and usually it's one of the first two or three that I'll want to use. A good producer will know how to curate beats which reflect you as an artist, but also manage to push you further than the path you've already trod. That's a special kind of relationship. They need to have an understanding of who you are, and what your ambitions are for your career. Emotional intelligence is such an underrated, but incredibly important, quality to have in a producer.

A rapper and producer will usually have different instincts for what makes a song perfect. In my experience, a producer tends to want the music to do more of the communicating. So maybe they want to layer up the instruments, make the melody a little bit more baroque, sit the vocals lower in the mix. And lyricists tend to be the opposite: they'll want to strip the whole track back, and pursue the purest possible interplay between words and sound. There is always a bit of back and forth, but it's not a fight. There's no hostility or anger, only passion for the art. It's like when you play with a length of wool in your hands to make a cat's cradle: it only works at all because there's pulling in two different directions. Without that tension, the wool would be slack, and the whole shape would fall apart.

The studio is the place for collaboration and experimentation. Your record will rise or fall based on how well you can work with other people. You've got to learn that being humble enough to take inspiration from other people's creativity isn't the same thing as compromising your vision. In the late 1990s, the biggest names in hip hop and neo-soul (Questlove, Erykah Badu, D'Angelo, Common, Mos Def, J Dilla and more) got together in Jimi Hendrix's old studio, Electric Ladyland. They called themselves The Soulquarians, but they never released an album under that name. Their approach was very, very playful. The Soulquarians treated Electric Ladyland like a clubhouse rather than a cookshop. It was a space to just mess around with samples, listen to music, work on a beat that another artist might chop up and use for something else. The principles of cooperation and healthy competition guided everything they did. They produced a lot of records together. Legendary ones: *Like Water for Chocolate*, *Voodoo* and *Mama's Gun* all came out of that collective. The space they built together was a haven for artistry.

So I like working with people who can recreate that kind of vibe: boundary-pushing and light-hearted, but seriously ambitious. It's funny that even when I'm in the studio working on the most solemn song, there'll still be a lot of laughter in the room. There's a real sense of social flow – we all understand each other very well, and on the best days, it's like me and my producer have a telepathic connection. I'll listen back to a verse and say something like, 'Can we try it again, but with a little less . . . ?' and they'll know exactly what I mean. If I say A, my producer will know I want B, without me having to ask. I don't have to find a lot of words to express myself – I can save all that for my bars! Sometimes I'll come home and feel bewildered that people can't read my mind in the same way outside of a studio. If I say A and my girl jumps to Q it's World War Z.

His & Hers

His and her point of view
In this world where we grew
There's his and her point of view
His and her point of view
In this world where we grew
There's his and her point of view
His and her point of view
In this world where we grew
There's his and her point of view
His and her point of view
In this world where we grew
Now here's his point of view

First of all I hate the way you talk to me
But I fucking can't stand when you're ignoring me
It's like every day you want to go to war with me
You're crying over spilt milk and trying to wipe the
    floor with me
Every time I ring you, your phone was in your bag
But every time I'm with you your phone is in your hand
Yeah, I get annoyed and you'll say I'm paranoid
Then I'll send another message like, 'I'll never phone
    you back'
And why would you say 'Cool' to that if you ain't cool
    with that?

You make me feel like it was all a plan
Like there's a man up in your yard
And you're waiting for the chance to let a couple hours pass
    just to call me back
And you don't never sound the same when you're in
    the wrong
Kinda sound like you're staring down your intercom
Just waiting for him to leave, said you'd tell me if you
    did cheat
And I'm breaking what we could be so I'm guessing it's
    make-believe
Still I don't believe you but I'll run with it
Cause I'm out 'ere keeping up some fuckery
And just because I beat doesn't mean that you can beat
Because two fucks don't make a right and it could never
    tarnish me
Sometimes I wonder if I've ever rocked your world
You care about your lashes and you care about your girls
The one you're always chatting, but she always does
    your nails
Talking about your fashion, 'It's gotta be YSL'
Even though I think the dress couldn't be shorter
Kinda makes me wonder, how the fuck were you brought up?
Hearing conversation about your love for the altar
Still I never listen cuh I've done it with all ya
At the end of the month I always give you money
And at the end of the night I always give you loving

Had to state a few things and you don't have to change
    nothing
It's just my point of view, I wouldn't tell you if it wasn't

His and her point of view
In this world where we grew
There's his and her point of view
His and her point of view
In this world where we grew
There's his and her point of view
His and her point of view
In this world where we grew
There's his and her point of view
His and her point of view
In this world where we grew
Now here's her point of view

I don't think that you respect me
I kinda think that you expect me to be here waiting for
    you cause its easier
Cause we've got a child together, went the extra mile
    together
But still there ain't a picture where we ever smile together
How many times do I have to say, how many times?
I'm getting sick and I'm tired and I'm tired and I'm
    crying my eyes out, I don't know why
And then you've got the cheek to come and dry my eyes

Avoiding me don't mean jack now
The toilet seat can go back down
And you can back down
You say your upbringing makes you never trust women
Well, it's funny how we're both from that background
And I trust you with my life
And you've hit me twice
And both times I came back crying
I wish you knew the kitchen just like you know women
I wish you knew the dishes just like you know whippin'
Between us there's a big difference, I might reply to a DM
    but you go the distance
Said I want a baby, you were scared, I could tell
But when you slept with that ho you weren't protecting
    yourself
And that's disgusting, imagine if you gave me something
Probably just say your favourite word, say nothing
And don't try and lie because I know that it's true
Cause one of your friends is fucking telling on you
Plus the fact I could fucking smell it on you
You treat me like I'd never do better than you
If you left me on the floor, that's a step up from you
I don't know why love made me settle for you
At the end of the day you know that you're my nigga
So at the end of the night I've always got you dinner
Had to state a few things even though you'll say I'm bitter
It's just my point of view, although you probably beg to differ

His and her point of view
In this world where we grew
There's his and her point of view
His and her point of view
In this world where we grew
There's his and her point of view

The Russian author Leo Tolstoy wrote: 'Happy families are all alike; every unhappy family is unhappy in its own way.' It's strange how we're drawn to writing about darkness more than we are to writing about light. There's something more cutting about it – an upbeat song can make you feel vicariously cheerful, but a song about grief or a break-up can put you right back in that moment. Maybe it's because we experience the memory of hurt in a different way to the memory of joy. Pain leaves a scar; happiness in hindsight is just the sadness that you don't have it any more.

For a long while I wanted to make a song like 'His & Hers'. As ever, I was just waiting for the right track. I suppose I didn't feel I had to rush it because I knew I was drawing from life; I was writing about something real and timeless. The inspiration came from one night when I met up with a bunch of friends after they'd been out to a club, like a little afterparty at the house kind of thing. It was a mixed group, guys and girls. I was late, and when I walked in, there was an argument in full flow. The battle line was drawn with women on one side, men on the other, and my mate and his partner leading each team.

My mate's girlfriend thought the waitress at the club had been all over him: 'When she came into the table section she'd only speak to you. She was whispering in your ear and playing with her hair.' And all the girls were in full agreement.

But the guys weren't having it. They were like, 'Bro, she was speaking to him because he's the one paying the bill. She was talking in his ear 'cause it's loud, and all she's doing is asking if we want more drinks.'

The girls were sceptical: 'Yeah, but did you see how she was when she put down the drinks?'

'She was just putting them on the table!'

'She was dancing as she walked up.'

'Because the music's on!'

'Come off it, what about when she came back when we were leaving . . . ?'

'She had the card machine!'

All this was raging around, and I found the whole thing quite funny because I'd been absent. But when I thought about it a bit more, I realised that if I had actually been there, I would've seen what the boys saw. The girls had a completely different experience of the night, and it was like they'd been at a different club down the road. It hammered home to me the power of perspective. I felt like I was in the middle of a crime scene and had to piece evidence from two different detectives together. Except one detective is in forensics, and the other is a psychic: they've got two wildly opposing ways of looking at the world, and yet they're trying to get to the same conclusion.

So because I'm trying to explore two opposing points of view, it made sense to structure it as a duologue, like a scene with only two actors on the stage. It's like a courtroom drama, with a witness for the prosecution and a witness for the defence each taking a turn on the stand. And you, the listener, are the jury. I kept the hook deliberately very simple: 'His and her point of view / In this world where we grew / There's his and her point of view . . .' It's a chorus in the truest sense of the word. In Ancient Greek theatre, the chorus were actors who narrated the play. They offered a bird's-eye view of the action, set the scene and foreshadowed doom – which is exactly what I'm doing in the hook of 'His & Hers'. I'm telling you the world that we're in and the theme we're exploring, and the repetition conveys the sense of a conflict which will never be resolved. It's not meant to be an easy song to listen to. In 'Cooked Food',

I introduced a note of darkness and then very deliberately pulled you back into warmth. But with 'His & Hers', you're left doubting whether men and women can ever see eye to ear, let alone eye to eye!

I knew I couldn't pull any punches with 'His & Hers'. If it was going to work, I had to think about things that I – and other men I know – have said in arguments, and the kind of things that women have said in response. From the man's perspective, I wanted every note of aggression to be undercut by a pulse of paranoia and uncertainty. 'First of all I hate the way you talk to me / But I fucking can't stand when you're ignoring me' is meant to be a powerful line. It's like a one-two combo, delivered with emphasis and purpose, and you're meant to be reeling from it – that is, until you realise it makes no sense. This is a man asking the impossible of someone: shut up and speak up at the same time. This is your typical insecure guy! He doesn't know what he wants, but he's blaming the woman anyway.

This is the telltale characteristic of the man's perspective: he gets the best rhetoric, but he's not necessarily in the right. The next two lines – 'It's like every day you want to go to war with me / You're crying over spilt milk and trying to wipe the floor with me' – are meant to have the tight and compact structure of a curled fist. The rhyme of 'war with me' and 'floor with me' links the two lines as a couplet, and the second one takes one idiom ('crying over spilt milk') and flips it back on itself by linking it to another common phrase ('wipe the floor').

This kind of poetic rhythm is known as *iambic*. One stressed (emphasised) syllable is followed by an unstressed one, so the rhythm is like a drumbeat urging you on. The rhymes are simple but the internal structure is complex: it's like he's trying to dizzy her with his verbal dexterity and the forcefulness of his words. He is making her entirely responsible for the conflict between them, and then saying the only reason she gets upset is because she wants to play the victim in order to destroy him. It's rational, but it's not reasonable.

The way his verse starts is so general that it invites you to see your own situation in theirs. Like, 'Oh, I really hate being given the silent treatment too!' The eight-bar that follows is a litany of all the petty bullshit that passes between them: she's ghosting on the phone, then using it to put emotional distance between them when they're together in person ('Every time I ring you, your phone was in your bag / But every time I'm with you your phone is in your hand'). The way he presents it, they're in competition to see who can be the coldest to the other. So he'll make a threat like 'I'll never phone you back', and she'll say 'Cool' to show she doesn't care. Even in very strong relationships, stuff like this goes on – people play mean little games when they're frustrated and can't find a better way to communicate.

But the real story in this verse is his paranoia. At first he brings up this emotion as though he's brushing it off ('Yeah, I get annoyed and you'll say I'm paranoid'). It's just another thing she says in order to discredit him. But look at how he starts spinning out in the time she's not picking up her phone:

> You make me feel like it was all a plan
> Like there's a man up in your yard
> And you're waiting for the chance to let a couple
>   hours pass just to call me back

She could be doing anything in that time. But maybe the reason she doesn't want to talk to him is because he's really hurt her feelings and she wants a bit of space. But instead of putting himself in her shoes, he chooses to interpret everything as a weapon she wants to use against him. It's not that he genuinely believes she's being unfaithful; he thinks she's so conniving that she just wants him to think he's being cheated on.

His response? Turn up at her flat ('And you don't never sound the same when you're in the wrong / Kinda sound like you're staring down your intercom') and accuse her of lying. Even here he's making a decision to interpret silence as guilt. He has no evidence of a man in there, he just construes discomfort at his turning up uninvited as damning evidence. Here the iambic rhythm serves the function of giving his theory of what's going on ('Just waiting for him to leave') and burying her insistence of her innocence ('said you'd tell me if you did cheat'). The way the emphasis falls means that you don't hear the words 'if' or 'did' as much as you hear 'tell', 'you' and 'cheat'. So even when he's reporting her words, it just sounds like a repetition of his own accusation. He's trapped in a vicious circle of his own creation.

The next four bars reveal the depth of his double standards. He's decided he can live with not having any trust in his partner, because he's out there cheating himself: 'Still I don't believe you but I'll run with it / 'Cause I'm out 'ere keeping up some fuckery'. Just let that sink in. The reason he doesn't believe his girlfriend isn't cheating on him is because he's cheating on her. It's the perfect example of him being rational ('I'm a cheater so I can't assume that everyone's faithful in relationships') without being reasonable. Because if he was being reasonable, he wouldn't have felt the need to turn up at her yard buzzing the intercom all night. He'd have just shrugged his shoulders and said 'fair enough'.

He's coming up with a whole set of justifications so he doesn't come across as a hypocrite. Instead of looking inwards and trying to find some insight into his behaviour, he just falls back on the bullshit that there are different standards for men and women: 'And just because I beat doesn't mean that you can beat / Because two fucks don't make a right and it could never tarnish me'. It's what we used to say to the girls, that a man can't be a slag. There is no word for a loose man. You wouldn't call him a tart, a slapper, a sket, a slut. It's always: he's a player, he's a gyalist, he's a womaniser. It's very complimentary for us. It makes you feel like you've won the Champions League! As boys growing up, we carried this sense that we could set the rules for girls but not have them apply to us. I would never face social consequences for sleeping around, whereas a girl would be seen as damaged goods, as though somehow less than what she was. As I got older I realised this way of thinking is a form of mind control. It keeps women in line, and lets men be men.

What I want to reveal in the song is that all of his macho and aggressive energy comes from insecurity. So immediately after his celebration of patriarchal sexual attitudes, he follows up with a moment of self-doubt: 'Sometimes I wonder if I've ever rocked your world'. And what makes him question his value as a man isn't actually the thought of her being interested in another man, it's her enjoyment of social spaces and things that are very girly: 'You care about your lashes and you care about your girls'. Which is quite funny, really. After all the fuss about cheating and 'a man up in your yard', he feels most threatened by the idea that she's happier when she's with her friends. He wants to separate her off from the people who make her feel like she's worth something. So he belittles all the things he says she cares too much about: nails, fashion, 'It's gotta be YSL'. He's making out that she and all her friends are shallow and amoral, because they go out and wear revealing clothes ('Even though I think the dress couldn't be shorter / Kinda makes me wonder, how the fuck were you brought up?'), and that it undermines her Christianity. But again, it's hypocritical. He's only saying it to diminish her self-esteem. He's brushing women off as trash because 'I've done it with all ya'. But if fucking him makes girls worthless, what does that make him?

I found the woman's perspective more exciting to write from. I like my songs to rise: so if I've got six flows in the first verse, there'll be eight in the second. It's all about building up to something. There's something about the challenge of stepping into another person's voice and trying to make it sound authentic: it forces you to challenge your own sense of self. There's a lot in that verse that's been said to me, and it made me reflect on how men relate to the women in their lives. The conflict, the blame, the balance of power. It makes you wonder whether you deserved to get your own way

as often as you did. Because I'm the kind of person
who can never lose an argument. If you give me a pound
and I lose it, I will spend the rest of my life trying to
convince you it was your fault for giving me it in the first
place. It's a very male trait. I don't think I'd ever need a
lawyer in court. I will just keep going and going, pulling
apart your argument, drumming in my perspective like
an iambic verse. Because I am(b) correct.

In order to heighten the emotional stakes, and also
just to make the woman's voice sound different to the
ear than the man's verse, I recorded the vocals twice.
Then I took one of those recordings, pitched it up, and
layered it over the first one. A lot of people told me they
found the sound of that vocal kind of annoying. But
that's the whole point! When you're arguing with your
partner, their voice takes on a completely different tone.
It's annoying, it's relentless, and somehow it sounds like
it's coming from the inside of your own skull. That's the
contrast between the woman's verse and the man's
verse. He makes his point in a way that you want to
believe, because it's put across in a way that you want
to hear. But the woman's voice is recorded in such a way
that you want to dismiss her for being nagging – even if
she's actually the one on the moral high ground.

He might get the one-two combo in the opening, but
there's a power in the bluntness of how she starts her
verse: 'I don't think that you respect me'. She doesn't have

to flex her rhetorical muscles to get her point across because the resignation in her voice in that one line conveys more honesty than his entire verse. The internal structure of her verse is much less rigid as well, with more flow between words than a strict iambic rhythm:

> I kinda think that you expect me to be here waiting
>   for you cause its easier
> Cause we've got a child together, went the extra mile
>   together
> But still there ain't a picture where we ever smile together

There's a lot more internal rhyme, and here the repetition builds up to an emotional crescendo rather than an argumentative point. Every time she says the word 'together', it emphasises just how far apart they are. While he uses idioms in an inventive way, there's a deliberate lack of verbal flourishing in how she gets her point across. She doesn't have to turn the kitchen into a battlefield to paint a portrait of their relationship; she just has to point out that after all these years they don't have any pictures where they smile together. That line has mirrored my reality at certain times: I had a moment where I looked back at significant relationships I've had, and couldn't think of a single image in which we were happy. And I want you to reflect on your love life in the same way.

It's very telling that she's the first in the song to bring up the fact that they have a child together. He'd been presenting her as being irresponsible: going out, buying designer clothes, toying with his feelings for the hell of it. But she's not just a girlfriend – she's the mother of his child, who's been there from the start. All that stuff about her being a bad partner looks different when you realise he can't even acknowledge being a parent. It casts their whole relationship in a different light, like maybe now they're fighting the fact that the love is gone and it's just a set of arrangements. You see it a lot with couples who've had kids before they were mature enough to handle it. They start taking the stress out on each other, and the kids are then front-row witnesses to the demise of their parents' relationship.

When I was writing her verse, I tried to convey the sense of a woman who's been pushed to the edge of her sanity because of how toxic her relationship has become. Again, this is like his verse turned on its head. He was rational without being reasonable, whereas her irrationality is actually quite a reasonable response to just how extreme her situation is. Rather than writing in a really tight and structured way, I chose to let lines run on into the next bar, so you get that sense of someone's emotions unravelling right in front of you:

How many times do I have to say, how many times?
I'm getting sick and I'm tired and I'm tired and I'm
      crying my eyes out, I don't know why
And then you've got the cheek to come and dry
      my eyes

Even though there are references to normal domestic bickering ('The toilet seat can go back down / And you can back down'), I'm trying to let you know through her words that this is not a healthy relationship. She's meant to sound hysterical. When she's talking about 'getting sick', it's not just that she's sick of him. The stress and the anguish of the relationship are making her ill. And that's part of what makes this verse so erratic, veering from theme to theme. But that looser structure doesn't mean her verse is devoid of wordplay. Instead of using creative language to convince him she's in the right, she's using it to illustrate just how absurd and contradictory their relationship has become. So when she says, 'And then you've got the cheek to come and dry my eyes', she's using the double meaning of cheek as having nerve but also literally drying the tears off her cheek, to demonstrate just how torn she feels about being comforted by the very same man who's hurt her. She doesn't get to deliver a knockout blow the way he does, because he's worn her down for so long. What she's experiencing is mental torture.

That's not to say she's entirely unable to recognise what's going on. In one compact pair of lines, she punches straight through all his sexist bullshit about one rule for him and another one for her: 'You say your upbringing made you never trust women / Well, it's funny how we're both from that background'. How can I trust you, but you can't trust me? We grew up as neighbours. Because it's often said that if you're a boy from a certain background, and your dad wasn't in your life, you'll grow up to have what's called 'a crisis of masculinity'. This basically means that you'll behave aggressively, find it difficult to commit to women, and generally lead quite a loveless existence. I always wondered why there's no such thing as a 'crisis of femininity': a girl who's raised in exactly the same circumstances doesn't get to use the excuse of her dad leaving for her behaviour.

But the unspoken thing here is that maybe she is carrying some emotional damage from being brought up in similar circumstances. They say that some girls who grow up without a father become women who seek from a romantic partner the love and security they never had. In 'His & Hers', her need to leave her boyfriend is only outweighed by her fear of being alone. She even says that the conflict between them has escalated into physical abuse:

> And I trust you with my life
> And you've hit me twice
> And both times I came back crying

It's the little words here that are the giveaway – 'hit' is in the past tense, but 'trust' is in the present tense. So in spite of him having punched her before, she's saying she still trusts him with her life. This says something about the lack of value she places on it.

Not only that, he's done it more than once, which means he's either incapable or unwilling to change himself. It's telling that she doesn't elaborate on the circumstances of this more. I deliberately didn't go into a lot of detail, because I wanted to show that in some relationships hurt and pain become so normalised that people don't even realise how big a deal it is any more. The fact that she skims over it and starts talking about the dishes is a way of showing how twisted the whole situation is.

A subtle undertone throughout the song is that she's in her flat the whole time. Her world has become so narrow that her horizons only stretch as far as him and the baby. Her home is a prison, with buzzers controlling who goes in and out. She doesn't even realise she has the power to leave, because he's always the one coming and going. That's why she pays more attention to the betrayal of cheating than the betrayal of violence:

> Said I want a baby, you were scared, I could tell
> But when you slept with that ho you weren't protecting
>   yourself
> And that's disgusting, imagine if you gave me something

Someone can only treat you as badly as you let them.

But instead of walking away she's trying for another baby, and he's scared so they're using protection. For her a baby means the promise of commitment, and that's why the cheating hurts even more than it would normally – he's not taking precautions with the girl he's cheating with! It's not that deep for him, but it is that deep for her. Even when she's calling him out, she's still giving away how much she's willing to put up with. Like, why are you still trying for a baby when he might pass on an STI or might get someone else pregnant?

The saddest part of this whole song is that both of them end on such petty notes. She says that if she was left lying on the floor, it would be a step up from him. And yet not only does she not leave, she then writes off everything she's been saying as 'just my point of view, although you probably beg to differ'. He says almost exactly the same thing earlier in the song. He still comes back with money every month; she still puts dinner on the table every night. That's why we come back to that looping and repetitive chorus. 'His & Hers' is fundamentally about a couple who are trapped in a cycle, eroding each other's hope for something better. This isn't the first time they've had this fight. And it certainly won't be their last.

I'm not trying to say that real love means never having an argument. But it always has to be a contest of equals, and it always needs to stay on a verbal level. There are no circumstances in which it's OK to inflict physical violence on a partner, or the kind of mental violence that means they can't even speak up any more. There's nothing worse than feeling resigned to being trapped in misery, and watching the same slow disintegration of the person in front of you as you feel in yourself. Bickering with a partner should feel like sparring with a worthy adversary. Their grip on logic and their verbal dexterity forces you to up your game, and there's something exciting about the idea that this person – and only this person! – could possibly get one up on you. That's how you know if you've met your match. Although you'd probably beg to differ.

In both 'Cooked Food' and 'His & Hers', I'm trying to show you the power words can have in shaping and breaking love. They're both songs which position the artist as being uniquely in charge of all the chaos and miscommunication that's generated when two people meet, fall in love and share their lives together. The difference between the two songs is that 'Cooked Food' doesn't take miscommunication too seriously. It's a joke which doesn't have anyone at the butt of it. It's a trick in which everyone can laugh. Whereas in 'His & Hers' you have the problem of two people who are talking a lot, but aren't able to comprehend what they're actually saying about themselves. They've lost sight of what makes a good relationship, they've lost sight of what's best for their baby, and they've lost sight of who they are as individuals.

I suppose that's the joy of writing love songs: you get to be the trickster, and never the tricked. You get to be the teacher, and not have to learn the hard way. But that's not always possible, either in life or in art. And in order to take your craft to the next level, you have to take the risk of getting a little lost first . . .

4.

THE WAYWARD SON
('UPON REFLECTION')

Upon Reflection

Reflecting, I reflect, I probably haven't been the best
I been away, I been depressed, been tryna raise you with
    a cheque
Now I could blame it on success and claim that I just need
Money, making up for lost time you can't get back on
    no Roley
In the morning cos we connect in ways in which we
    haven't done
I pray them school runs would turn into a marathon
It's funny how I always work from home but don't get
    home from work
It's funny how I pray you grow and work but don't get
    home for church
Now I'm reflecting through my sentences that's just a
    lonely verse

I made a promise in my foreign whip so that I won't
    reverse
Now I'm speeding down memory lane
Running out of petrol almost every day

Reflecting on how I treated every woman that I sexed
And now my daughter's nearly ten it's like I've found my
    common sense
I guess it's easy to regret, like it's easy to finesse
But now I finally got the message, I can cc all my friends
Now we got kids the same age, we used to roll the whole day
We got older and then we went our own ways
We ain't spoken in a minute but you been on my mind for
    hours
When it's all said and done it be written in loads of flowers
On the coffin
You been my nigga since when we were cottin'
First tooth, first coupe, first college
First zoot, first move, first bondage
First bar, 32, verse honest

Reflecting on how I'm treating all these members of
    my family
You a friend or you my family? It depends on if you just turn
    up to the Grammys
And you didn't have a shoulder or a brandy
When my show was half full in the Academy

Embarrassed to come out. When there was holes up in
 my couch
At home playing cat and mouse, there was rodents in my
 house
You said I never had drive but now you're wanting
 chauffeuring around
I reflect on my reflection, will I make it to my pension?
I had a bottle at my entrance, will a bottle be my exit?
It's ironic that's symmetric, pour me another death wish
While I drink it, will I perish from a shot or from a beverage?

Too much reflecting
Too much reflecting
Too much reflecting
Make a mirror crack
Seven years' bad luck now, yeah
Hate your reflection
You're still looking back
Wishing for what you had
Didn't know what you had
Don't break the mirror

I reflect on my career, I think about the wonder years
See once I went to Number 1 all other numbers
 underwhelmed me
Top 10 just left me feeling like a failure
Top 20, now you feel like euthanasia

You're heavy-breathing in the label
When they're waiting to exhale you
You think you've had your heyday and they feel they're
    Tony Bellew
All the diamonds in your ring that had you dancing
    like a girl
Grew me nothing, there's something that your
    disembowelled you

Pray for the change to come
It came and it's changing ya
No way was a chain enough
Cause the paper keeps changing up
Pray for the change to come
It came and it's changing ya
No way was a chain enough
Cause the paper keeps changing up

I think about Chip from time to time
The truth is we both made a difference in our lives
And it's petty that we couldn't put those differences aside
We left it under troubled water and the bridge is still on fire
All those times you reached out to have a talk on it
I wasn't really ready for no walk on it
Same brother, different mother, same orphanage
But when you're from a broken home, you shouldn't
    auction it

Closed doors turn into revolving doors
The Internet just made the world smaller. They don't
    even own a business
But involved in yours
Staring at a meme with an open jaw
Reflecting on my teams there was Photoshop
And nobody was Photoshop.
Still everything was crystal clear
Without scrolling through a thousand pictures
Waiting till they disappear
Focus. Now you're out the room, but your kid's in there
The real Black Mirror's here

Too much reflecting
Too much reflecting
Too much reflecting
Make a mirror crack
Seven years' bad luck now, yeah
Hate your reflection
You're still looking back
Wishing for what you had
Didn't know what you had
Don't break the mirror

Every musician has an internal EQ level, or emotional intelligence: there's technique, there's madness, there's imagination. And a genius tends to have all three turned right up to the maximum. I wouldn't put myself in a high madness category, but there have definitely been times when I've strayed off the straight and narrow mentally. What's more, the experience of success itself changes the balance of your artistic EQ. You see people go through their careers turning the technique up, and the madness down. You mute your inner rule-breaker, you stop wanting to experiment. That's how musicians turn into mathematicians. Or maybe exposure to fame, and everything that comes with it, increases your madness but kills your intelligence. Imagination without technique to bring it to life is just a pipe dream. The fact is, there's no straight road in success – an artist walks a wayward path.

That's what this chapter is about: getting lost so you can find yourself. And you'll find a verse in here that you won't find anywhere else. 'Upon Reflection' is about taking an unflinching look at yourself, all while maintaining that sideways glance at the world which makes your artistic perspective unique. Throughout these pages you'll find discussions of madness, conflict, isolation, loss. Because lyrics never tell you how you to get from A to B. That's not art, that's just instruction. Narrative is the thing that happens when life takes a detour, and you feel a disconnect between what's happening and what was intended. That's what I'm reflecting on, and perhaps also suggesting that the act of reflection itself involves straying from well-travelled roads.

When you're naming the song that your album shares a title with, you agonise over it. It's like naming your child, only they can't change it by deed poll in twenty years' time! The smallest changes can make the biggest differences; a subtle shift in emphasis can change how you view the whole album. I went back and forth over whether to call this track 'Upon Reflection' or add an 's' at the end. Because something as little as turning 'Reflection' into a plural transforms what I'm talking about entirely. Suddenly there's this added layer of distance: I'm not just thinking twice about something, I'm casting my attention on what it means to think at all. When you turn something into a plural, you're inviting different voices to come in and tell their story as well. And while there are songs where I'm just the vehicle for other people's perspectives ('His & Hers', for example), here I wanted to write something really intimate and personal. I settled on the singular 'Reflection' because I'm trying to share my point of view.

I started this song with a very simple question: how do I sum up what this album is about? And the simple question produced a simple answer: I'm making a connection between how my circumstances today (being a father to a daughter, my present success) make me reflect upon my old wrongdoings. What's the difference between reflecting and regretting? Both involve returning to your past. In my opinion, reflecting is wanting to own it – regretting is wanting to change it. There's no erasing what's already been done. No one on this earth has that power.

Of course, there's always room for remorse. But remorse is about healing the present so you can change the future; regret keeps you trapped in the past, reopening old wounds and wondering why the pain refuses to fade. What I'm trying to say with this album is that I've accepted everything that's been a part of my journey, and by sharing it with my audience, you'll be able to jump over the hurdles that tripped me up. 'Upon Reflection' is therapy for me, and training for you.

A word of advice: the simplest task is the hardest to get right. When you write a duologue like 'His & Hers', or even just any track that goes verse, chorus, bridge, the blueprint for what you have to do already exists. It's like trying to build a skyscraper versus creating the illusion of floating. You need to feel solid in your choice of words, even as one phrase flows into the next, and the verse melts into air. You need a lot of internal scaffolding so no one sees where you're touching the ground.

Some of that structure comes through repetition. So the repeated refrains of 'Reflecting' and 'I reflect' are both a thematic and a poetic building block: it sets the tone in terms of content, but also in rhyme. I use an assonant 'eh' sound throughout to hold the song together even as the specific topic and tone shift. But there's also an undercurrent running through the song: that question of why I don't feel as close as I should to the things and the people that I love. In psychology, you'd call that *emotional affect* – the persistent pulse of feeling that underpins everything else. The way this song is structured is meant to feel cinematic, like I'm standing in front of a mirror and instead of my own reflection I'm seeing the faces of all the people I wish I could talk to. It's a montage, really.

The sense you're supposed to get is that you're seeing through my mind's eye. It's a bit like that opening shot in *Roma*, where you see the sky and a fighter jet reflected in splashes of mop-water on a tiled floor. The setting of the song isn't in physical space, but in my own state of mind. It's the kind of track which comes from sitting down in the studio, just listening to the beat and digging deep. I'm looking for emotional significance, and not just what I think people want to hear me speak on. Which I suppose is why I've ended up talking about lows rather than highs. How do you become who you are? How does anything evolve? You're not the culmination of all your best moments, you're the product of your mistakes. If that's good enough for Charles Darwin, it's good enough for me.

You actually have to be braver in a song like 'Upon Reflection' than you would when you're just flexing. There are no boasts, there's no ego, there's no character to hide behind. You cannot flinch from saying difficult things. So I start the song by addressing the people I'm most afraid of having hurt: my children. And not flinching away from what I have to say comes in direct conflict from that natural urge you have as a parent to protect them from any and all pain. But here I'm saying that 'I probably haven't been the best' because I haven't been as present for them as I could be. I've been parenting at a distance: 'I been away, I been depressed, been tryna raise you with a cheque'. And I suppose it's something a lot of parents can identify with: you're working all the time, maybe not even in the same country, and your children start to see you as more of a stranger than a carer.

But if I'm honest, there's a different thing going on with me: 'I *could* blame it on success and claim that I just need / Money', but that's not the whole picture. The truth is that being an artist creates distance between you and the people around you. As mad as it sounds, because it's so abstract, I'm always closest to the art. When everything is an opportunity for a verse or a song, you're living life just a beat out of step with everyone else. You're an observer, not a participant. And when you want to be world class at something, it takes time. Time away from your kids, time away from your loved ones. It's a sacrifice. To master anything you've got to put in 10,000 hours. Think about how much you miss in 10,000 hours. And to become the greatest, you have to put in ten times that.

The act of drawing from life changes what you're drawing on. So if I need to spend ten days locked in the studio, with no one hearing from me, that's going to impact my circumstances when I pop my head back up again. People feel abandoned, or confused. I might have been writing love songs in there, but that's not going to be the same situation now I'm out. You can't just ponder on something and expect it to stay still. That's the impossible task of an artist – you're trying to capture something that's in constant flux, and the time you take to make the work is time during which the thing you're depicting is changing. So I'm writing songs for my kids, but because I'm doing that I can't watch them grow.

It's weird to explain, but as an artist, you can't sit right with complete happiness. If you're going to write a song about pain, you need to put yourself in a position where that is what you're feeling. And that's dangerous! But I'm always looking to unlock new versions of myself, new ways to say things, and that means opening myself up to all kinds of experiences which might be damaging. There are times when I was at my busiest, and my work was just about being tired – I'd go out and find love just to put that feeling in a song. Or maybe a certain person had a weird effect on me years ago, so I'll get back in contact with them. Every life decision is subordinated to what I can create from it.

And that's tough on my family relationships. There are those moments I wish could stretch on for ever ('I pray them school runs would turn into a marathon'). We're driving, and my daughter's surprising me with how sharply she observes things, and I don't want the moment to end. I look at both of my kids like they're a wonder. And then the car door slams, they're running off into the playground, and I'm alone again. You start asking yourself questions when the thing you love to do takes you away from the people you love the most. I'm not sure I'll ever find an answer for it.

Conversations aren't always the best way of communicating. Think about all those times you regret saying something, or you walk away from an argument with things you should have said still bubbling up inside of you. The French call that feeling *l'esprit de l'escalier*, the spirit of the staircase. It's that moment when you're stomping upstairs and you slap your forehead because you've finally got the perfect comeback and the other person's already out the door.

But when you're writing a song, you have the luxury of time. I'm the kind of person who wants to express themselves right the first time and every time. If I have an argument with my girl on the phone, I'll hang up and write down what I'm thinking in my Notes app! I need to be understood, and I need to say exactly what I mean. I like having time to refine my words. So making a track, if gone about correctly, is the ideal way of resolving tensions with someone. It's all there in black and white. Take from it what you will.

There's no one person to blame for the distance between me and Chip. It's not like either of us set out to do the other any harm. We used to be proper close, I saw him like my lil bro, and still do. 'Same brother, different mother, same orphanage' refers to our shared origins. It's funny, 'blood is thicker than water' is one of the most misunderstood phrases: it actually means the opposite of what everyone thinks it does. It doesn't mean that your relatives are closer than friends: it means that the connection between your chosen 'blood brother' is a more powerful tie than the 'water' of a 'birth brother'. And that's what I'm saying with that bar. Tottenham was a cradle for our creativity, but it was also a place where you had to learn to look after yourself very fast. In order to survive, you create a family of your own choosing as well as the one you were born into.

But when you're both on the same journey, and things happen at different times, you need to be able to accept that the game is a roller coaster, and you're in control of when your career takes off. So in the beginning, I was in a position where I could help Chip. Then a bit later, he was in a position where he could help me. But by the time things had evened out and we both attained the level of success we have now, communication had broken down a fair amount. It's not that there were huge blazing rows between us: the problem was the frost, what wasn't being said. When there's only something small to go on, you tend to assume the worst out of self-protection.

The problem when you both have a profile is that you stop seeing each other as people. If you don't stay alert to it, both the man you are and the man you knew turn into a name. There are all these people and whispers getting between you, and suddenly you're not talking to each other but around each other. Maybe you're not as warm or friendly as you would normally be when you bump into each other. So what happened with us was when we finally did get around to talking, there was a whole backlog of things weighing down on us. Of course, it doesn't help when one or two stupid tweets are thrown into the mix. Then your situation becomes food for public consumption. You've got to realise that when it comes to beefing on social media, you're never the butcher, you're the meat on the menu.

Saying someone's name in a song can either cut through the noise or set off an explosion. With something like this, how it turns out depends on how thoughtfully you chose your words, on whether the other person is willing to listen to what you have to say as well as what they want to hear. But I think Chip gets what I'm trying to say with this. I also wouldn't put it out without sending it to him first: with rappers you're always wrestling with what they actually meant, trying to grapple with subtleties, but I don't want to encourage any misconceptions here. That's what I mean by 'when you're from a broken home, you shouldn't auction it' – we share similar backgrounds, so I'm not going to try and prolong a conflict just to get more sales.

'Upon Reflection' is the anti-clash. It's not about spitting fire, it's about shedding light. If I didn't make music myself, I'd probably want artists to clash all the time. But as a rapper, I can see that the pressure of a clash is both so appealing and so frustrating. It's an extremely rare thing to get everything perfect in one moment, and that's why there's always back and forth between clashing rappers. The way I see it, if I have to say something more than once, I've failed. Even though Jay-Z is 100 per cent my guy, I think every diss should be an 'Ether': a one-punch knockout. Because when you let something persist on and on, it stops being about the people directly involved in the conflict. The only happy people in battle rapping are the fans. We'd all gladly pay our £49.99 pay-per-view to watch Anthony Joshua and Tyson Fury box a hundred rounds, but that doesn't mean it's the right thing to do. They could kill each other. They could be left paralysed for good. And for what, just to satisfy our appetite for fighting? It's a dangerous thing to keep stirring up a beef just to keep a reaction going, because where will it stop?

I realised this when Ghetts was clashing P Money. There was a back-and-forth of songs, and in my own (biased) opinion I thought that Ghetts' material was the superior out of the two. Game over. But when I spoke to him he was like, 'Nah, man, every time P Money puts a tune out people are @'ing me and now I've got to respond.' I was like, 'Bro, you should be spending this time working on your album! Don't stop your recording sessions to do this.' You're never going to stop people from crowing at the sidelines. You can only stop yourself from throwing them breadcrumbs.

There's a difference between healthy and unhealthy competition. Ronaldo and Messi spurred each other on to greatness, but it's not like one was looking to tear the other's ligament any time Real Madrid came up against Barcelona. The idea of the clash is that in order for you to be victorious, the person you're up against should have no more listeners.

It didn't feel comfortable to me. Some people thrive on hostility, like maybe it gives them an adrenalin rush or something. And there's a format and a place and a stage for that, but there's a difference between being a musician and being a battle rapper. I don't like setting out to use my skills in such a negative way. Being a writer is like getting a degree in anatomy: you can use that knowledge to become a doctor, to heal and uplift people, or you can use it to inflict maximum damage.

Because that's what you're doing in a clash: you're trying to assassinate someone's character, pull them apart and beat them down until they can't get up again. There's always pressure to escalate – go harder, cut deeper. And that means you're constantly mentioning names and dragging in other people, who don't even need to be involved in the first place. It's a house of cards, and you're trying to scramble to the top by pulling other people down – as if the whole thing won't collapse on top of you all.

When I say, 'I reflect on my career, I think about the wonder years', I'm not just talking about myself. I'm thinking of the ones who came before me. I remember seeing various rappers in the class I came up with, churning out all those hits. Someone starts low in the charts, then grafts his way up to Number 3, then he gets the crowning glory of Number 1. And then he puts out an album and gets to top-selling male. He's riding the high off that, his achievements are incredible. Then when he comes back, his singles are still charting high, but not breaking the Top 5. Everyone is looking at him thinking, 'Oooooh, that's tough.' There's this sense that he's slowly falling. Which, when you think about it, is mad. Getting a Top 10 is only falling because he's been to Number 1! So he's caught in a situation where he's only a failure by the measure of his success. I always wondered how other artists felt about that.

And then fast-forward, it's happening to me. Except in my case it was more of a surprise because an artist like me was never meant to get a Top 10 single. But even though it was a measure of worth that I'd never expected, I felt that gut-punch after. I felt like I wasn't hitting a bar that I'd set for myself. And it makes you lose your sense of joy in what you've achieved – like how are you supposed to celebrate coming second in the charts if you topped them last time? I reckon that feeling is a major player in what tips artists over the edge. It's not just what you're exposed to in terms of fame, it's about the value system you internalise. You've got this gnawing sense of failure chomping away at you inside, and your perspective gets distorted.

That's why I had to put that theme in 'Upon Reflection'. What I'm doing in this song is the flip side of braggadocio: in something like 'Punctuation', I'm telling you how I'm the best, and how no one can touch me. But here it's about how being the best gives you a constant fear of losing your status – 'once I went to Number 1 all other numbers underwhelm me' is that moment of standing at the top of Mount Everest, and realising the only way is down. The emphasis on 'you' in 'euthanasia' is deliberate: it's Superman saying he's scared he's losing his powers, and he'll just be an ordinary man in the crowd. It's the fear of making the journey from audience to centre stage in reverse.

The difference between me and Tinchy is that I'll rap about that feeling: I'm not the kind of guy to pretend there's nothing happening. The artist thing to do is acknowledge vulnerability when you feel it, and take the power away from those who are trying to keep you trapped in a game that inevitably you'll lose at. The little 'heyday . . . Tony Bellew' pun is a comment on not putting yourself in a position where you try and fight the same fight as you used to, only to get knocked out by the new up-and-comer.

The person who understands this best is Jay-Z. A few years ago, we all saw him as invincible. He was powerful, he was wealthy, he'd built a position of prestige in the industry that no rapper ever had before. His branding was immaculate. And while he could have just kept growing his investment portfolio and building up Tidal, there would have been no way he could have developed as an artist. And then, that footage leaks of Solange in the elevator. And even in that moment, he does the right thing – doesn't hit back, still the coolest head in the room. But then Beyoncé does *Lemonade*. For another man, the outcome could have been a total retreat from public life altogether. Or just the worst humiliation, of trying to carry on like before while everyone whispers behind his back.

But instead Jay-Z released 4:44. He owned the narrative. He puts out this album where he addresses all the things that had been unsayable before: cheating on his wife, shooting his brother, celebrating his mother coming out. He tears down the image he'd created for himself, and holds up his hands to admit that he's a deeply flawed human being. And not only does he manage to reinvent himself as an artist, he reconnects with his audience. Because how is an ordinary person meant to relate to someone who is very nearly a billionaire? You need to see the scars, the chinks in his armour. In any case, I prefer seeing armour with dents and scrapes on it. You know that it's worked.

There's a limit to how much vulnerability you can put in a single record, though. Because you want to convey that sense of being overwhelmed by your thoughts ('Too much reflecting, too much reflecting') without the whole thing becoming unwieldy. You have to look coldly at what you've created, because the edit might make it better. You have to weigh up the cuts – are you trimming a fingernail or the finger? If it hurts, you know you should keep it. But I didn't feel that way here. So I ended up taking out this verse, purely for structural reasons:

> I reflect on my reflection, will I make it to my pension?
> I had a bottle at my entrance, will a bottle be my exit?
> It's ironic that's symmetric, pour me another death wish
> While I drink it, will I perish from a shot or from a beverage?

It's a shame it didn't fit in the track, because this is a moment in the song where I've gone from reflecting on how I've treated other people, to reflecting on how I've been treated and how I treat myself. Here, I'm not just thinking it's time away from my family that creates distance: it's success itself. Because when you grow up without very much money, and suddenly you start making piles of it, things change. Some of those changes are good – I can give back to those who gave to me, make them feel appreciated and special. But there's a darker side to it too. You start questioning whether someone wants you around for what you mean to them, or what you can do for them. Because there are people who just want to be around for the good times. You'll never lack company at an awards show, but what about when you're struggling? There were people who looked at me when I was broke and thought that what was in my bank account was a reflection of what was in my heart. That I wouldn't amount to anything, that I didn't have drive.

This is the part where I can't duck the fact I'm talking about my own situation. When I'm talking about my kids or women that I've been with, it's still general enough so that other people can identify with it. But when I'm talking about feeling 'Embarrassed to come out' when my show is half full, there's no hiding. And again, it's the kind of thing musicians don't feel they're allowed to talk about – that creeping fear that your audience aren't interested, and you're performing to a disappointed crowd. The rhyme of 'out' with 'couch' creates a connection between my past and my present circumstances. Like deep down, I'm scared that professional failure will mean going back to feeling stuck and having nothing.

And I don't just feel precarious because of other people around me, or how my audience reacts to me. I know I have a self-destructive side. I've never been into hard drugs or anything like that, but I know that alcohol can be a risky one for me. And it's everywhere. 'I had a bottle at my entrance, will a bottle be my exit?' is thinking about how my birth was celebrated with a bottle, that it's on my rider when I tour, and if I don't stay in control, it could be the end of me as well. So many artists have lost their way trying to find their message in a bottle, and I doubt many of them could identify the exact moment it became a problem. So as long as you're drinking, you're playing with something that could easily overpower you. I went from nearly being hit by a bullet when I was nine to doing shots every night as an adult. There's a word in psychology for this: *Thanatos*. It means you're drawn to things that destroy you as much as things that bring you pleasure. So I'm literally drinking my own death wish.

I wouldn't be the first artist to drown out their words with alcohol. Addiction was the shadow that haunted Billie Holiday, the morning-after rasp in Amy Winehouse's voice. In hip hop culture especially, alcohol is connected with death. You pour one out for the fallen. And yet, for all its morbid connotations, alcohol is part of celebrating your success. Think about how often you hear references to champagne, Henny, Cîroc. I think the artist who understood this duality best was Gil Scott-Heron. You listen to a tune like 'The Bottle' and the vibe of the track itself is so intoxicating that you forget he's singing about the way alcohol abuse tore through black communities in the 1970s. He even asks the listener to look out on 'the corners' because the brother looking like 'a goner' could be him.

That was one of his most popular songs, played at clubs and block parties, and on it Gil Scott-Heron is opening up about how he is in thrall to addiction. That capacity of honesty is the mark of true artists. It turned out to be a prophecy: Gil Scott-Heron was one of the greatest lyricists who ever lived, but in the end his life was lost in the bottle.

One thing that 'Upon Reflection' is getting at is the idea that fame itself is dangerous. And that's why artists are fascinated by it. It's not just that we're trying to articulate our immediate circumstances. Once more, it's about the pull towards something that has the capacity to annihilate you. You can see it with Kanye West: fame is like a fire that he's drawn to, and he can't stop touching it. He's obsessed by fame. At this stage, I don't know how much Kanye is left in Kanye. It's the nature of being a creative. He gives, gives, gives, and we take, take, take: whether it's the new album, the new Yeezys or the new outburst. We're taking advantage. When Ye said, 'No one man should have all that power', I knew exactly what he meant. Once upon a time you were the fan going to concerts and book signings, but now all the fans are coming to see you. You go from zero to hero – but with each new album to create, you lose a little part of yourself. Think about how much Kanye had created by the age of forty-one. After nine solo albums – not even counting his collaborations or work as a producer – I'm not sure how much man is left in the man. Fame burns when it touches you; it damages your soul. It's not something that everyone's able to adjust to.

Back in pirate radio times, you felt like a star on those occasions when someone would come up to you and say they'd taped your set. That was our measure of success. The yutes today are all used to instant feedback. They put their song up on Instagram, or on YouTube, and the comments are immediate. But when we were doing pirate radio, we didn't even know if anyone was listening! Sometimes you'd have put your heart and soul into a set, and it'd turn out that the fucking aerial wasn't in place or something, and you were just rapping into dead air. The only way you'd know something was wrong would be if someone rang you up in the studio: 'Hey, bruv, I'm locked in, but all I can hear is fuzz.'

If I wanted to, I could quit music any time. Once you get to a certain level of having a profile, you can just rely on being a brand: partner with a clothing company, do a few photoshoots, live easy. I wouldn't have to tear myself open every other year to make an album cataloguing my worst mistakes. But while there's lots of things in life I've tried my hand at, that I enjoy and feel I'm good at, rapping is the only thing I've ever felt passionate about. That I want to be the best at. I know that if money didn't exist, and capitalism ended tomorrow, if views on social media were invisible: I would still be rapping. That's how I know I'm in love with the music, and not the fame. If you locked me up in a prison cell, far away from the world, I would still be writing bars.

There's a difference between someone who's invested in the art, and someone who's just a moth. It's never sat well with me that sometimes people are just drawn to the spotlight. I'll meet a genuine supporter who wants to talk about an album, or a lyric that really resonated with them, and they'll ask to take a picture – but then someone else will come up and interrupt, saying, 'I don't know who you are, but let me take a picture!' It's like they think I'm just a monkey at the zoo, and it's OK to crowd round the cage and get me to perform for a photo. It's dehumanising. I'm not a commodity – I'm a warm person, and this is just acting cold. 'Are you famous? Can I get a picture?' I always just shrug my shoulders and gesture to the other guy: 'I dunno, he just seems to think I'm someone for some reason.'

I never wanted that shit. That's why every opportunity I get, I run to the shadows. If I have to suffer, I'll suffer in silence. But I've always been a loud and funny kind of character. I was the class clown in my early years! I was used to the spotlight, so I didn't mind so much when it magnified. It's a scary thought: one day things could get so big that there's nothing I can do, or nowhere I can go, if I want to hide. How far is too far? I guess I'll know when I get there. I think Kanye's in that place. He suffers in volume. That's why I don't pay much attention to the shit he says, about Trump or slavery or this and that. I just think we should sit back and enjoy the music, or the trainers, or whatever it is he's created for us.

People having their heads wrecked by fame isn't anything new. But what's different now is social media. Don't get me wrong, I love it as a tool. I can use it to enrich my audience's appreciation of my music, share little bits and pieces with them. But that's what it should be – a tool and not a weapon. And right now, it's firing in all directions and it doesn't discriminate between celebrities and civilians. It's like everyone who's got Twitter or Insta is a celebrity on a promo run. They're under pressure to perform and keep up appearances, no matter what they're going through at home. And if they melt down, they'll melt down with an audience.

That's what I mean when I say 'The real *Black Mirror*'s here' in 'Upon Reflection'. The dividing line between technology that could make a utopia and something that brings about a dystopia is very, very thin. What was meant to be a tool to help us socialise has created an environment where the opposite happens. People use it to hurt and to troll. If you can't write your post and then put your phone down without thinking about it, then you're in a bad pattern. I think it's especially dangerous for musicians. Because your fans can become your enemies in a heartbeat. Everyone's got their opinion: maybe they really liked track seven on your last album, so now they're angry when not everything is like track seven. It's corrosive to creativity. And everyone wants different things, so you end up feeling pulled in different directions. Eventually you'll have no flesh left on you.

Everyone who has a social media account needs to ask themselves where you draw the line between giving enough and giving too much. I've always erred on the side of caution, and that's probably to do with being a bit of a control freak when it comes to expressing myself in public. I'm not afraid of speaking personally – I mean, that's my whole career – but I want to minimise the room for backchat and misinterpretation. Whereas

Twitter basically begs the world to take your comments out of context, to cause a big drama. And it's so easy to forget there's a person at the centre of that social media storm. With my music, I won't let you forget there's a real human at the heart of it.

Maybe this awareness comes from not being a 'digital native'. Like, I can remember life before social media. Not having the Internet on your phone, just a brick which maybe had *Snake* on it if you were lucky. But it's a completely different story for my kids' generation. It's like they were born with an umbilical cord and a 4G connection attached! They're saturated in social media, and it can be very damaging at an age when they're incredibly vulnerable. Think about it: any teenage girl with an Instagram account can be subject to the same kind of nastiness and viciousness about her looks that a multimillionaire actress is. There's always been bullying, but now it can literally follow kids home and into their bedrooms. Its inescapable.

I read about this really tragic case of a teenage girl who took her own life. She'd been posting about depression on social media, and even after her death, the social media algorithm was still recommending graphic images about self-harm and suicide. That's some real *Black Mirror* shit, and parental controls aren't enough to protect your kids when that's the kind of system that apps automatically operate on.

So it's not enough for me to be aware of how dangerous social media can be: I'm out of the room, but now my kids are trapped in there. It's frightening. They're growing up in a setting I was too grown to get bogged down in.

The funniest things can make you realise the fragility of mental health. It doesn't have to be a massive crisis moment either. My realisation came when I was in Jamaica with my bredrins, and we'd just been to the Bob Marley Museum. I saw these Rastas selling weed cake on the street, and I thought I'd buy some for everyone. When in Rome, right?

At first, everything went according to plan. I was laughing, my bredrins were laughing, it was all good. Then something started happening. I was in KFC and all of a sudden I was like, 'Rah, I can't stand up.' I was on the floor, thinking, 'Fuck, I cannot move.' It took a long time, and all the while I'm just willing myself to get up, repeating the instruction over and over in my head. Eventually, after what felt like decades, I got to my feet.

We decided to head back to the hotel. And as soon as I got out of the car, another wave of weirdness washed over me. Despite having stayed in that hotel for six days, I couldn't remember where my room was. I just thought of all those identical doors on identical floors, and felt a flutter of panic in the pit of my stomach. I turned to my friend Whitney and asked her to take me to my room, and she herded me up there like a Sherpa through the Himalayas. At last we made it to my room and I lay down on the bed and looked out the window. I don't know why, but there was something weird about that. All I could think was 'Why the fuck are you looking out the window?'

Another flutter of panic. Just as Whitney was about to leave the room, I asked her to stay. She told me to sit up and drink some water, and I realised I couldn't even sit up! It was like I was trapped, with all these mad thoughts whirling around this head of mine. The left side of my face started feeling funny, and I was like, 'Oh my God, I'm having a stroke.'

So now I'm really freaking out. Whitney's called everyone into my room, and I'm about ready to recite my last will and testament. I'm crying, everyone else is around my bed crying, and I'm so convinced I'm having a stroke it's like my mind has tricked my body into feeling the symptoms. And all I can think is that I need my phone in my hand, so I can FaceTime my kids while I can still speak. I was telling people that I had to tell my children that I loved them, because I might not ever get the chance again. Who knows how I'd recover after a stroke? I needed to tell them everything about life that's important to hear. My friends were just like,

'There's no way we're letting you FaceTime your kids in this state. It's one in the morning, for God's sake.'

By this time, the hotel had got involved and called an ambulance. I was put on an IV drip, and I'd lost track of how long this had all been going on for. If you've ever had a bad trip, you'll know what I'm talking about: the fear, the glitches, the loss of coherence. I remembered all the people from my neighbourhood who had gone mad. They'd spent their whole lives smoking skunk and it had permanently altered the chemistry in their brains. And the more I thought about how their lives had turned out, the more I felt a resolve strengthen in myself: *this is not going to be me.*

And I started repeating to myself, 'You're coming back.' It felt like a wrestling match: on one side was the weed in my system, trying to prise my own mind out of my grasp, and on the other was me trying to claw it back. I know it sounds funny, because it was just a bit of weed cake, but I'm not used to feeling that out of control. It was the first time in my life that I saw the edge of my own sanity. The abyss was right there. It was a proper scary one, and it took every ounce of my strength to pull myself back from it.

But if an experience of weakness can lead you to your strength, the opposite can be the case too. It's like the Bible story of Samson and his hair: it was the source of all his power, and his downfall came when it was taken away. That's how I felt when a period of success led to me being held back from releasing music.

This all happened when I was coming to the end of my contract with Ministry of Sound. When I'd signed the deal, they predicted I'd sell 40,000 albums without any expectation of a hit single, and hopefully we'd get to silver. But then the first single dropped and it got to Number 5. Which was great – except that meant the goalposts had moved. The label started cranking up the pressure: 'Do what you did again, and maybe we can get to gold.' And then I did it again. And again. And then when *Black and White* dropped, it got to gold.

So where do you go from there when it comes to the next album? I had in my pocket a record that was true to what I wanted to create – challenging, with hardly any choruses. So immediately there was a problem with the label, because all they wanted was me to just make the same album again. But how can you make the same album twice? You can't force yourself back into the same headspace as you had the last time around.

It became a stalemate. Ministry wanted the hit singles, but I wanted to release what I'd made. I'm a businessman too, so I understand that if you have an artist who can make a Top 10 single, then that's what you want them to do all the time. That's where the conflict came from. The label wanted me, but it wasn't the me I wanted to be. Like you might have long silky hair down to your waist, but one day you might want to cut it all off. And your partner will tell you they actually only really liked you with all that long hair. They don't understand that you're still the same person – they'll still be getting you, only with an added dose of Halle Berry. It's take-it-or-leave-it time. It went back and forth and a rift opened up. I managed to Frank Ocean my way out of it.

Everyone on this earth has a reason for being here – and for me, it's because I've got music to make and I've got something to say. So that period when I couldn't release the album, I could feel something happening. Sadness. Emptiness. Worthlessness. What's an artist without his audience? It's like a doctor without any patients. I felt like I didn't have any value. That's the feeling I'm talking about in 'Upon Reflection', when I say: 'You're heavy-breathing in the label / When they're waiting to exhale you'. When you're signed to a label, it's like they're dictating whether you can breathe or not. When you're contractually locked into the wrong situation, not even having control over the quality of your own output, it can be the most disempowering feeling in the world.

If you saw me at that time, it's unlikely you'd have thought there was anything wrong. Maybe I was just a bit quieter than normal; but mentally I was in a dark place. I live on my own, so I found myself alone at home a lot, deep in thought. I couldn't understand why I wasn't just going out and making music. Why I couldn't shake this feeling of dread. I would spend the days pacing my floor, wondering if I was losing my mind. I'm used to being the guy who's supporting other people, who's lifting them up when they need someone to rely on. But who was going to do that for me? I'd try and speak to people and they'd play it down: 'Ah, you've got your career. You're still performing. You've got your money. You're easy.' Everyone just assumes that the carer is cared for.

Earlier in this chapter, I talked about how each artist has their own internal EQ levels. Technique, madness and imagination. So what happens when your speaker gets turned off? It's like having your entire sense of purpose taken away from you. It's not insanity, it's lifelessness. I knew that this thing I was in was dangerous; I wasn't trapped in madness per se, but I was a prisoner of my own success. I was at my lowest when I wrote '6 Words'. I knew I was capable of writing songs that could connect with a mass audience, but I won't do it just because that's what the label expects of me. I like doing it when I want to do it. If I do it when *you* want me to, I'm not being organic – and the song's not gonna sound authentic. I'm an artist, not Deliveroo.

You can't just snap your fingers for a pepperoni pizza and have me winging it to you in thirty minutes.

That's the irony of being a writer. In order for you to maintain your integrity as an artist, you have to have total creative control over what you put out. But the creativity itself exerts a certain amount of control over you. There are moments when you're no longer tapping into feelings in order to make art; the art itself is taking over your feelings, and transforming you from the inside out. In 'Upon Reflection', the very perspective which allows me to comment on my life and the world around me is the thing which deepens the sense of distance between myself and the things I love the most. Think about it: when you touch a reflective surface, the first thing that you feel is cold.

But I needed that cold in order to create a song which could communicate feelings of warmth. I'd been sitting on the concept of '6 Words' for a long time: 'I can't sing but I wrote you a song, yeah'. And that day, at my darkest hour going into the studio, I knew the time was right to make the idea a reality. That opening line is about the lengths you'll go to in order to show your devotion – like 'I know I'm no good at this, but for you I'm willing to give it a go.' So there's a doubleness there: my label put me in a position where I couldn't sing, but I wrote them a song anyway. And then I left and released the next album on Polydor. I'd lost my voice, and ended up writing a song that even the bar staff will sing along to at my shows. Out of loneliness and isolation came a moment of real collective joy and togetherness. It's weird, because I wouldn't have been able to get to that chapter of my story without having gone through that experience of not even being able to turn the page.

Of course, certain characters had to enter the narrative first . . .

5.

THE FATHER
('HUSH LITTLE BABY', '6 WORDS', 'MUMMY'S BOY')

In this life, you are born three times. The first time, obviously, is when your mother brings you into the world. Another is your first brush with death, which is what I talk about in the 'Soldier' chapter. The most transformational of them all, however, is when you become a parent yourself. And that's what this chapter is about: the lost son being reborn as the father.

So far, this book has talked about life stages purely in terms of artistic development. I've tried to show that no artist begins their craft fully formed. You're constantly drawing from life, and that process of depicting what you're living changes your circumstances as you do it. But this chapter is a little bit different: I'm talking about how my children turned my whole world upside down. It changed how I write, how I think, and even how I remember my own past. After my kids came along, my work changed. It's like you can see their smudgy little fingerprints on every record I've made since. Because at that moment in the hospital, it wasn't just my child who was born. It was a new me.

Before I had my boy, I was a clever lyricist but I wasn't a thoughtful one. I didn't really think about the responsibility I had as a rapper to my audience; I kind of thought that as long as they enjoyed the work, that was all that mattered. Then after he was born, I started thinking about life differently. So that sense of being a bit more reflective began naturally to affect the music as well. I reflected more deeply on the messages I convey in the work. And once I had my daughter, I considered what my overall message about women was like in my work. You can't disrespect the life you've just produced! It's a very deliberate choice that I made, to make sure no one is spoken of in a brighter light than my gran and my mum. It's so important to show that it's two women at the top of the pantheon for me.

I wanted to make sure the overall message was positive. Like sure, there might be one line or one song where I talk about wanting to sleep with a girl. But that's not the whole picture. In a lot of rap, women are presented as always wanting to take something from a man. They're bitches holding you back, or they're demanding commitment that you don't wanna give, or they're hoes using sex in exchange for clothes and clout.

How is it that men will depict women as wanting to take without giving, when it was a woman who gave you life in the first place? Who put shoes on your feet and food on the table? Next time you want to say that a woman is too clingy, just remember that for years you cried every time your mum went into the kitchen to make herself a cup of tea.

Think of this chapter as the closing of a loop. If you have kids yourself, hopefully there's a lot in here that you can relate to. If you want kids yourself, perhaps you'll be able to use this as a map when it's your time to navigate the path. And if you don't want kids, just use this chapter as a way to vicariously explore the road you never took. You'll get a peek into what it's like to become a parent, without the worry of saving up for uni fees. I'll start with the moment of finding out I was going to be a dad ('Hush Little Baby'). Then I'll talk about the feeling of growing into that responsibility ('6 Words'). And finally, I'll go back, to the parent who taught me how to be a parent in the first place ('Mummy's Boy').

Hush Little Baby

Hush little baby, don't you cry
I said hush little baby, don't you cry
I said hush little baby, don't you cry, no
I said hush little baby, don't you cry

I'm saying hush little baby, don't you cry
Daddy ain't sure if he can raise you right
I ain't even good with saving my money
Why should I think I can save your life?
And the whole family's gonna think I'm a devil, I don't
    wanna see my angel's eyes
I say this with one hand on my heart, guilt ain't gonna
    make me change my mind
My first thoughts were the worst thoughts, running
    round my head in circles
The world's gonna hate me for saying this, but patience
    is a virtue
So we don't have to rush for our first yout, we can take
    time, do rehearsals
And I ain't acting, this is personal, and I ain't doing
    this just to hurt you

I should say goodbye, before I say hello
So darling, hold me, closely, tonight
Because if you open your eyes, I'll never let you go

Moving slowly, we'll both sleep tonight
And we'll just be dreaming till you wake me up

When I'm telling her about raving
She's telling me about cravings
I want her to just get the message
I don't wanna have to be so blatant
So I told her my life ain't balanced
Yeah, said the time ain't right
She said God's clock's the only one that matters
And it's about time I tried, yeah, and if I listen to my family
Then there'll be a new addition to my family
I can't help feeling peer-pressured, everybody's looking down
  but they don't understand me
And everyone's so suggestive, I'm getting mixed messages,
  but nobody's rang me
Huh, I'm saying this ain't a game, but I say the wrong thing
  everybody wants to hang me

I should say goodbye, before I say hello
So darling, hold me, closely, tonight
Because if you open your eyes, I'll never let you go
Moving slowly, we'll both sleep tonight
And we'll just be dreaming till you wake me up

Hush little baby, don't you cry
I said hush little baby, don't you cry

I said hush little baby, don't you cry, no
I said hush little baby, don't you cry

I know I should say goodbye, before I say hello
Darling, hold me, closely, tonight
Because if you open your eyes, I'll never let you go
Moving slowly, we'll both sleep tonight
And we'll just be dreaming till you wake me up

There aren't many songs I've been scared of my children hearing. My general rule when it comes to music is that if something is truthful, then it must be right. There is no higher law than being authentic to yourself. But there are moments when your honesty as an artist comes into conflict with your commitment as a parent never to bring any harm to your children. 'Hush Little Baby' is a song about doubting whether or not you're ready to bring a child into the world. And because in order for the work to feel honest, I had to recreate that moment of real internal struggle when I found out my girl was pregnant, my fear is that my son will listen to it and think I didn't want him. At times I wonder if it was selfish of me to record the song at all – it's not like he was old enough to give permission for me to put it out there.

But when the art says yes, you can't say no. When the

idea comes knocking on your door, you can't stay in with the curtains drawn. For me, the genius in Lauryn Hill's 'To Zion' wasn't just the giddy, love-struck chorus dedicated to her son; it was that she included the lines articulating the battle between head and heart; balancing advice on what's best for her career with her desire to become a mother.

I remember listening to that and thinking to myself, 'Rah, who said to concentrate on your career, the Devil?' Because the person talking to Lauryn isn't just saying that her career's important. They're saying that continuing on her professional trajectory means that she shouldn't continue with the pregnancy. The fact that she was able to include a sentiment so dark in a song that would stir the spirits of 99.9 per cent of mothers out there helped give me the courage to say what I needed to say in 'Hush Little Baby'.

I was twenty-one when I found out I was going to be a father. And even coming from an ends where most people had to grow up quicker than they'd like to, it still felt like a massive shock. It was before I'd put out my first album, I was in the middle of putting out *Learn from My Mixtape*, and my life was in a state of flux. The first line of the first verse – 'I'm saying hush little baby, don't you cry / Daddy ain't sure if he can raise you right' – is right in that moment of uncertainty. It's a part of my story, and I can't shy away from it. So in order to really face up to my fear, I opened the song as though I was addressing my unborn child and telling him all my doubts. I'm trying to say the unsayable – because lots of people will talk about feeling daunted by the responsibilities of becoming a parent, but very few will talk about what that actually means. The question up for discussion isn't really 'Can I cope?' It's actually 'Should this child live?'

That's why I try and set out what the stakes are in the following lines: 'I ain't even good with saving my money / Why should I think I can save your life?' The use of the word 'save' across two bars sets up a contrast between the immaturity of perspective, and the gravity of the decision that's in front of me. Like, 'I ain't even good with saving my money' is the kind of thing a teenager would say. It's as though you're telling a yute who can't stop raiding his piggy bank that now he's got to put down a deposit on a house. There's a little note of defensiveness in the wording of 'Why should I think I can save your life?', as though I'm placing the blame on my unborn baby for putting me in this position in the first place. It's not meant to sound reasonable: the choice I'm grappling with at this moment is whether or not I can justify denying a child a chance to grow because I'm scared of growing up myself.

As the emotion builds throughout the verse, the object of my address starts slipping and shifting.

I transition from talking to my unborn son, to playing out a conversation with my family in my head. It's like I'm doing that thing of anticipating how an argument is gonna go, and rehearsing my ripostes in advance: 'And the whole family's gonna think I'm a devil, I don't wanna see my angel's eyes / I say this with one hand on my heart, guilt ain't gonna make me change my mind'. The question the listener has to ask is whether someone who genuinely thought they had nothing to feel bad about would insist: 'guilt ain't gonna make me change my mind'. I'm using a technique called *apophasis* here, where you say something by denying that you're saying it. It's like when someone says, 'I've got nothing to apologise for' – deep down, you know they're being eaten up by regret. So it's not quite as straightforward as me just saying what my family would think of me if they knew I was considering asking my partner not to go on with the pregnancy. There's also an undercurrent of viewing myself through my family's eyes, in order to express the feelings of shame that I'm not allowing myself to confront directly.

The state of mind I'm trying to convey is that of a clever person who isn't thinking straight: 'My first thoughts were the worst thoughts, running round my head in circles'. It's a very dangerous thing to have intelligence without insight. Because when you've lost your sense of right and wrong, you still have an ability to construct an argument that could win people over. It's like being a lawyer, and representing the Devil in court. So again, the person who I'm arguing with changes. In the song, I keep moving the goalposts, chopping and changing who it is I'm trying to convince.

Now, I'm talking to the woman who's carrying my child:

> The world's gonna hate me for saying this, but patience
>   is a virtue
> So we don't have to rush for our first youth, we can take
>   time, do rehearsals
> And I ain't acting, this is personal, and I ain't doing this
>   just to hurt you

These bars need a little bit of unpacking. In a similar way to when I'm talking about what my family would think, I'm anticipating what society would think about what it is I'm going to say. They would hate me for talking so openly about something that still carries a lot of stigma even in this day and age. But I'm also trying to deliberately convince someone of my point of view now. In previous bars, it was like I was backing off from the argument by being defensive from the get-go. But here I'm actively trying to be persuasive. I'm turning the language of morality on its head. By saying 'patience is a virtue', I'm invoking biblical language to suggest that the moral thing to do would be not to have the child and live life without having to face up to the responsibilities of my actions. So rather than rushing headlong into adulthood, we can take a little time to live our 'first youth' and rehearse for a child rather than actually raising one.

The connection of 'rehearsals' with 'I ain't acting' in the next bar pulls the verse back from mere rhetorical flourish. While I'm utilising linguistic skill to persuasive ends, ultimately it's rooted in a very real emotional conflict. I'm not just flexing for the sake of it. The words of the chorus, coupled with Ed's performance of the vocal, is pure yearning. It's about the push and pull that you feel as the doubt fights against this new love that's starting to grow:

> I should say goodbye, before I say hello
> So darling, hold me, closely, tonight
> Because if you open your eyes, I'll never let you go

Because the love you feel as a parent is unlike anything you feel elsewhere in your life. It's biological. It's written in your DNA. So in this chorus, I'm struggling against the inevitable. I'm trying to suppress what I know is right in my heart.

I can't generalise for an experience that I'll never have (for obvious reasons), but I think that physical, bloodline connection of love between parent and child starts earlier for women. So in the second verse there's a disconnect in communication. It's like we're in different time zones or something: 'When I'm telling her about raving / She's telling me about cravings'. Her focus is internal, on this massive change happening to her body, whereas my priorities are being out in the world and partying. But again, if I'm being honest on the track, I can't flinch away from a truth that doesn't make me look so good. Talking about raving is a vehicle for something coded: I'm trying to tell her that maybe she shouldn't go through with the pregnancy because there's a whole world that we'd be missing out on ('I want her to just get the message / I don't wanna have to be so blatant'). The irony is that because I'm so focused on what we could be missing out on, I'm actually failing to see the magic of what's happening right in front of me.

When I performed the song on Radio 1, I remember being asked by Nihal if I was worried what other people would think when they heard it. And honestly, I was like, 'Nah.' Because I know from experience that just because you feel something dark, it doesn't make you a monster. I think most people who become parents have at least a split second where they wonder if it's the right time. Doubt is the emotion that distinguishes humans from animals. It's something that we can experience, because we're always haunted by the futures that could have been. The problem is people don't discuss this stuff openly. Normally when you've been on the precipice of making a decision that's wrong, you try and erase the memory of being in that moment. But the bottom line is you have to submit to the art. When you set out on the path to be a writer, you can't suddenly decide that you're gonna hold back now. Your life belongs to something else. It would be like waking up one day, and deciding that you're just gonna stop loving your children. It's physically impossible!

I don't know what it would be like to hear this song from your dad when you're ten. I hope my son sees more positives in this song than he does the negative. I want him to hear it, for him to understand me better, and for us to be brought closer together. Maybe one day he'll be teetering on the edge of parenthood, and the song will make him feel understood and empathised with in his moment of doubt. It's a milestone in life when you first realise that your parent didn't just hatch fully formed from under a rock: your dad was a boy who had to grow into a man. He's human, and he's made many mistakes. But none of those mistakes was having you. You were a gift. He might have helped bring you into the world, but you taught him what it was to live in it.

★

6 Words

I can't sing but I wrote you a song, yeah
Wrong notes but the melody's so clear
When I'm lost, I'm still close to gold 'cause I found my
    treasure in you
And that's priceless spending, now let me count my blessings
1 life, 2 children
3 time, 4 dreaming
5 senses, 6 words
I found my treasure in you
And that's priceless spending, now let me count my blessings
1 life, 2 children
3 time, 4 dreaming
5 senses, 6 words
I found my treasure in you
In you
I found my treasure in you

Bronze, silver, gold . . . no, it's you
I found my treasure in you
Nothing less than that will do
'Cause I found my treasure in you

I can't sing but I wrote you a song, yeah
Wrong notes but the melody's so clear

When I'm lost, I'm still close to gold 'cause I found my
    treasure in you
And that's priceless spending, now let me count my blessings
1 life, 2 children
3 time, 4 dreaming
5 senses, 6 words
I found my treasure in you
And that's priceless spending, now let me count my blessings
1 life, 2 children
3 time, 4 dreaming
5 senses, 6 words
I found my treasure in you
1 life, 2 children
3 time, 4 dreaming
5 senses, 6 words
I found my treasure in you

Bronze, silver, gold . . . no, it's you
I found my treasure in you
Nothing less than that will do
'Cause I found my treasure in you
I found my treasure in you
I found my treasure in you

I can't sing but I wrote you a song, yeah

If you ask an artist what the smartest song they've ever written is, you'll always get an interesting answer (and never the one you expect). Because when you ask that question, you've already got a certain set of parameters in your mind for what makes a song smart. Maybe you're looking for an immensely intricate track, with dozens upon dozens of samples layered up to create a rich and shimmering texture. Or maybe the thing you value above all in a song is lyrical dexterity, so the song that embodies intelligence the most for you is something with dizzying wordplay, elaborate metaphor, breathless delivery. But the artist is looking at that question through a different lens. If you're Beyoncé and your fans know you for hitting every note under the sun, maybe the song that excited you most was when you got to rap. For Wiley, who's celebrated for spitting like a machine gun, his smartest song was 'Wearing My Rolex' because of the way crowds would sing it back. And in my eyes, my smartest tune isn't an 'Antwi' or a Fire in the Booth. It's the simplicity and serenity of '6 Words'.

Without a doubt this is one of the most important songs of my career. '6 Words' is my 'Isn't She Lovely?' A lot of people don't realise Stevie Wonder is actually singing about his daughter in that song. And it's similar with '6 Words': it's a song that people get married to, that they listen to when they're falling in love or celebrating their anniversary, but they don't know that the 'you' in the song refers to my children. Don't get me wrong, I'm not complaining about it! The beauty of a song like '6 Words' or 'Isn't She Lovely?' is that it can work on two levels. The first is understanding it in the light of the specific thing I was writing about; the second is when the music resonates with something you're carrying in your heart, and you can project your own situation onto the lyrics. Because basically, if a love song doesn't specifically reference sex or raving, as a parent you can use it as a vehicle for how you feel about your kids. And this song is an opportunity for the listener to take that same journey, but in reverse. Think of it as an invitation rather than an imposition.

There's a bit of an edgy flip side to '6 Words' as well. I've already talked about how I recorded it at a time when I was at my lowest. But there's also an aspect to how '6 Words' fits in with how I view myself as an artist. Because don't get me wrong: I have a love for the craft, but I'm a mad competitive writer as well. It's not good enough for me to only measure myself up against people who happen to be in the same genre or scene as me. That's like saying you don't want to be the best chef, you just want to be the best at cooking rice!

I always want to break out of whatever box someone puts me in. I see my competition as Chris Martin, Kendrick Lamar, Ghetts, James Fauntleroy – people who I think have in some way ripped up the playing field and changed the game. So for this tune I'm not actually taking inspiration from rap or hip hop. I'd been listening to a lot of Take That. I was asking myself how Gary Barlow would go about writing a song, and picturing the crowd's reaction if it was playing at Wembley Stadium. It's not about copying exactly what they'd do. Because you do sometimes hear songs which clearly are trying to recreate what's been done before. The radio is full of Poundland Ed Sheerans and Lidl Adeles. That kind of thing leaves me very cold. Instead, my approach was to think about how they channel a personal sentiment through music to create a collective moment. That's the irony at the heart of '6 Words'. It might be a love song, but actually I was being just as competitive as I would if I was clashing!

I wanted to prove I can do more than just string words together. Songwriting is a very different discipline to rapping. When you're rapping, you're always layering meaning on top of meaning. You can never just let a phrase go – you take it, you play with it, you turn it inside out and you squeeze every possible interpretation from it. So when I'm working on something more melodious like '6 Words', I make sure I have a writer in there with me to stop me from adding too much. They're on hand to help strip out the connective tissue: no 'ands', 'buts' or anything else that links clauses together. I had to learn that singers don't do that – they let the music speak through them. When I first sent '6 Words' around, there was a bit of a hoo-ha because people didn't believe it was me on the track: 'Aren't you gonna rap on it?' That's how I knew I was doing the right thing, because it's when you confound other people's expectations that you know you're growing as an artist.

I had the concept of the song from that first line going around my head for years. 'I can't sing but I wrote you a song, yeah': in my mind, it was like the opening words of a film. In a single bar, you've got a whole story. I'm a rapper who's deliberately not speaking in the form he is strongest at. It's about vulnerability, the lengths you'll go to to demonstrate your love for someone at the expense of all your ego and bluster. There's nowhere to hide. It's just me, my untrained voice and the sentiment. It's meant to be selfless, a parallel to how people are when talking about being in relationships. Like, 'I don't know how to do this, but I'm doing it for you.' I'm scared of heights, but let's go to the top of the Empire State Building. I can't cook, but here's your favourite meal. The intention at the heart of the gesture shines through the imperfection of its execution ('Wrong notes, but the melody's so clear').

When I first came up with the opening line, I didn't know what would follow it. All I knew was that I had to tap into an emotion that felt very real and very honest. And that's when I clocked that the feeling I was conveying was actually how I felt about becoming a parent – totally unprepared, out of my comfort zone, but willing to try because of what I felt for my kids as soon as I met them. Love is an alchemist. It can turn heavy lead into bright gold.

I deliberately structured the song so that it was very looping without being clunky. The way it's put together is meant to reflect familial bonds across generations: the images and metaphors flowing across the lines in a way that mimics love pouring from parent to child. The challenge of the song was being able to convey meaning with as few sentences as possible. Because when you think about it, I make '6 Words' all the time. Except it normally takes me a million words and permutations until I feel I've nailed what I'm trying to say. And it's a hard discipline for a rapper to train themselves in. Normally the craft is all about maximalism – everything is rapid, verbose – and this is the complete opposite of that way of working. It takes a clever mind to do more with less, to seek out refinement over magnitude. And the end product – the texture, the vocal – is a bit weird. But it's the obvious flaws which encourage the listener to relate to it. It closes the distance between artist and audience.

Just because the song embraces straightforwardness, doesn't mean it's absent of technique. In fact, you've got to be more thoughtful and editorial about how you use linguistic flourishes to enrich the meaning, and not distract from the feel when you're trying to do something very simple. I used a technique called *dinumeration*, where you list off points one by one. Usually you'll see this in a piece of persuasive writing or an argument, but the quality I wanted to convey here was more like weaving a spell:

> And that's priceless spending, now let
>   me count my blessings
> 1 life, 2 children
> 3 time, 4 dreaming
> 5 senses, 6 words

This is the sentiment that makes amends for the moment of doubt I had in 'Hush Little Baby'. Instead of worrying whether being bad at saving money is worth losing a child, I talk about the time I spend with my kids being priceless in comparison to what it costs. It's like I'm an accountant, weighing up matters of the heart. It took some tinkering to get right, like initially I was saying 'I love' instead of 'I life'. But had I phrased it that way, people would've felt I was talking about being in love with one person rather than referencing the Bob Marley song. It all fell into place when I came up with '5 senses'. I proper chuckled to myself when I got that line, because I could feel it take the song up a gear. It was what took '6 Words' from being just a love song to something that felt like a proper celebration of how my children give my life meaning. It was like realising that the purpose of your senses is to show and teach the world to the next generation.

The culmination of the song is of course the six words that the hook builds up to: 'I found my treasure in you'. There's no complicated reason for why this phrase works. There's not some obscure poetry term that make sense of it, it's not an ancient rhetorical device. It's just human. Everyone can identify with treasure. It's what civilisations were built on. And in every single culture, poets and writers compare what's precious to them in their lives to what's considered precious in society. I'm still flipping it around here: 'Bronze, silver, gold . . . no, it's you'. It puts the love I have for my children on a pedestal above any material value. It also takes a little nod at Olympic medals, and places them as the achievement that's my crowning glory – head and shoulders above any other kind of validation of my career.

Beyond all the plaudits and all the sales, nothing brings me greater pride than the fact that my kids love this song. They love the video, they love knowing it's about them, and ultimately that's the most positive review I could've got for it. My son and my daughter each have a plaque for the song, so they'll always know they were part of its success. That's priceless spending, 'cause I had to pay for it! It was an especially eye-opening experience for my daughter, because she was that bit younger when it came out. It was one thing to know that Daddy wrote a song about her; it's another to hear it on the radio in Mummy's car, or see it on the TV when she gets home from school.

However, I do think I topped this song with 'I.O.U.', but because of label politics it wasn't a single and it didn't blow up the way it could have. If anything, the hook sung by Emeli Sandé is even simpler! And as it's basically a homage to my mum and my big sister, the song is really close to my heart. It's important that my family gets to hear exactly how I feel about them in my work, when my work is something that takes me away from them. Luckily there will always be another song, and another album, in which I can get that message across.

Mummy's Boy

Oh they try to burn me
Call me Mummy's Boy
Say I'm girly
Well, he's gone and built a house
Guess I'm Hercules
Worldly, call my mama 'Zeus'
'Cause she's worthy
Hercules, call my mama 'Zeus'
'Cause she's worthy

When I look in the mirror I see my mummy, boy
All my four different sisters look like my mummy, boy
See now I work for a living 'cause of my mummy, boy
'Cause she was handling business when I was unemployed
When I took a turn for the worse I needed my mummy, boy
Tell the truth, I just wanted to hear 'I love you, boy'
What a world of a woman, that's just my mummy, boy
And now I worship my woman 'cause of my mummy, boy
I been conditioned to better my living conditions
Five women I grew up with gave me strong vision
Became the man of the house and replaced the
    man missing
That's when you saw mummy's boy and saw there's a
    dad in him

'Mummy's boy' all you want
'Cause this mummy's boy's all she's got
We got stronger every time we lost
It's like she stirred courage in that corn beef pot
Yeah

Now I got a daughter and she's daddy's girl
I tell her she's important 'cause she's daddy's girl
I'll hold you together in this shattered world
Social media won't affect you like the man himself
Think I gave a fuck about opp
When my daughter had an op
Had a feeling in my heart
But if she needs it, then I'd swap in a second
I'll put me second, hoping I can make it to heaven to see my
    bredrin
They can never question my character 'cause I fell for
Someone that resembles a character of my
    world, you're
Out your mind if you get the shivers and you ignore it
You only live once, I was tired tryna enjoy it
By myself. I needed help with all this wealth
Already had a million girls, a million sales
You're only as low as you fell, as high as you felt
You need faith, it's no Biggie, Diddy can help
Uh

I been feeling like myself lately
Hearing children that are really tryna imitate me
When I'm one of one, not one of many
If they're claiming they're 100 to 1, it's just gotta
    be pennies
Tell the country that they can count on the son to be
    magnetic
Pull you closer and then be picking you up, it's just
    calisthenics
Being helpful – that's a trait from my mum
Get in pole position, that's the Formula 1
Still I drove you up the wall, borrowed your car
Breezed from the constable
Still you tried to defend me, rather they put cuffs on you
Probably do life twice over to see I'm comfortable
That's why I'd give my life twice over to give you life support
There's suttin 'bout a woman
We just think about putting our suttin in a woman
I tell you that there's power in empowering a woman
'Cause every time I fell, I got picked up by a woman so . . .

I hope the crown don't weigh you down
I'll pick you up if it does
You built the throne on your ones
At home trying it on, in hope to become like you
I hope the crown don't weigh me down
You'll pick me up if it does

I'm on the throne on my ones
All soon ready for my son,
Fit for a king just like you
I hope the crown don't weigh me down

I've never understood why the term 'mummy's boy' is seen as an insult. People use it as a way of saying someone's soft, that they're feminine, that they're not tough enough to make it on their own. It's so weird to me, because I owe everything I've achieved to the decisions my mother made. That's what this song is about: giving her the celebration that she deserves. In poetry, you'd call this a *panegyric*, a verse in praise of a person. It's normally something that got written about kings and queens: so obviously my mum belongs up there with royalty! But because this panegyric is from me, I had to put a spin on it: taking a negative word, flipping it, and making it positive. So in that first verse, I rely on two techniques. The first is *epistrophe*, which employs repetition at the end of a sentence: the use of the words 'mummy' and 'boy' throughout the first verse to really hammer home that I'm talking about a parent-and-child relationship in which I'm looking up to my mother. And the second is *anhorism*: this is a redefinition of an imagined opponent's term so that a word meets my purposes. Normally you'd hear 'mummy's boy' used to insult someone. Instead, I'm framing it as the highest compliment you can pay a man.

Explaining this song properly needs more than just technical analysis. It's not a guide to verse you need, it's a telling of my family history. Because it took leaving the protection of my mother's house for me to start taking my career seriously, to grow up and become a man. But I still couldn't get to the point of understanding my parents – the strain they were under, some of the decisions they made – and see them as human beings operating within constraints, until I became a father myself. Because it's easy when you don't have that sort of responsibility to judge your parents more harshly than they deserve. You have to realise that they never wanted to pass their pain on to you; they only wanted you to get their best, and to learn from their mistakes. I could only develop that awareness once I took a step or two in their shoes.

To be honest, I've never really had an in-depth conversation with my parents about how they got together. I know my mum and dad went to the same school – William Forster in Tottenham (which then turned into Langham, and then turned into Park View). From what I gather, my dad was quite a ladies' man. And my mum was *the* lady, even though she was very young. She was only sixteen when she had my eldest sister, Elaine. I came along in 1985, the year of the riots, joining another sister who'd got a head start on me. There's more of my mum in the older children, for some reason, so Elaine and my mum are practically identical. There's more of a mix in me. I have good relationships with my siblings. Some I speak to a lot, and some I don't speak to very much. But we've got good relationships in silence. We get on in different ways.

I can trace my musical side back to my dad. He was a DJ, and the records he kept in the house were my musical education. Lots of dancehall, lots of reggae. I remember being little and seeing the hi-fi in the living room, in a glass cabinet that I wasn't supposed to touch. A little magnetic click where it closed, and all these buttons that I didn't know the purpose of. I always felt it had some kind of spiritual significance, like a shrine in the house for the purposes of worship. It's my dad who's responsible for the most formative moment in my career; not when I got signed, or my first Top 10 single, but the moment when I knew this is what I wanted to do.

He was DJing one night and took me with him.

Instead of leaving me to watch from the crowd, he brought me behind the decks. I was standing looking over his shoulder as the dance floor pulsed with his every command. It was amazing, seeing how his charisma and expertise gave him power over a whole club. That was when I knew I didn't just want to be entertained: I wanted to be the entertainer. I had this in mind when I brought my kids out at V Festival in 2015 after performing '6 Words'. My boy was standing there, soaking up the crowd's roar; my daughter was a little intimidated, and stayed curled up tight in my arms. I was thinking about how I'd felt when I saw my dad work his magic, and I wanted them to experience that same moment.

My dad showed me what it is to have a love for music. You're not just up there as a personality, you're letting something move through you. During my childhood, things were pretty eventful. Dad was living with us on and off, and my younger sister had half-siblings (twin brothers) in the same year as her at school. It never felt like a big deal at the time, but now looking back I can see it was a lot to grapple with. I feel that one day, I want to write a song from my dad's perspective – to put myself in his shoes, and make sense of all that went on in my childhood. It's not about pinning the blame or making anyone feel demonised. Instead, I want to find the humanity in decisions that were hurtful. To make sense of how one person's choice can affect a whole family. The upshot of it all was that my mum was effectively a single parent from early on, raising five children. And that made her a soldier.

Let me tell you a little story about how strong my mum is. My younger sister, the one who came after me, was actually born in the house. No ambulance, no nothing. I remember one day my mum was in the kitchen, and she turned around and announced that her waters had broken. I rang 999, but by the time I got off the phone it was already happening. Mum was in her room coaching my older sister through helping her with the birth: 'Elaine, when the baby comes out, you've got to hold the head up.' And then the screaming started . . . The next time I walked back in the room, the baby was there. But she was silent, not crying. My dad got back to the house just before the ambulance, so he was the one who smacked Mahkedar on the bum and got her lungs working.

I was about six years old when all this happened. I had no clue what was going on, I thought my mum was dying and I kept phoning the ambulance again and again to see if they were any closer. I didn't fully comprehend just how tough my mum had to be to get through that situation. As an adult, I'm now thinking, 'Rah, you didn't have no gas, no painkillers, and no adults around you?' I'll never forget her face when the ambulance came and they put her in the wheelchair. I was sitting in the living room, and as she was wheeled past she turned to me and gave me a look, eyebrows raised and an exhausted puff of air out of her cheeks. Like, 'Yeah, that happened!'

It's crazy to think that for most of human existence on earth, that's what childbirth was like for women. Why would you even want to get pregnant? Women are so gangsta. Imagine if someone said to me, 'You can play these nine games, but on the tenth you'll break your leg.' So I know when I'm playing this game, that excruciating pain is coming for me. I might just stop around game seven. Or I might not even start! If men were the ones who had to give birth, I guarantee the human race would die out. I heard recently about a guy who was watching his girlfriend give birth to their first child, and as he was watching all the screaming and the blood, it suddenly struck him that every woman he'd ever slept with was taking the chance of this happening to her. He got this urge to ring them all up and thank them personally, like, 'Thanks for taking an insane risk on an absolute shmuck!' The fact that women are willing to go through all that multiple times is just bedazzling to me. Stupendous. You all deserve a medal for that alone.

Women having to make a sacrifice doesn't end after the child is born. They're the ones having to run the whole ship, while getting none of the credit. That's why I could never let my kids get away with being rude to their mum or to me. If I hear so much as a tut, it's 'Get back here!' from me. In terms of discipline, I'm like my mum. I have this thing with my son: I ring him more than he rings me. It bugs me when he doesn't call me. I wait to see when he'll ring me, but then I remember he's a kid. I used to do the same to my dad. And often he wouldn't call either, so I guess I'm similar to my dad in that way. But when it comes to discipline and morals, I take after Mum. Because after seeing what she went through to bring my sister into the world, I'm making sure my children are raised to respect the people who created them.

I understand so much more now than I could back then. When kids go back to school, for example, it's 'buy new school uniform time'. I only have to worry about two, but my mum had five, and she was on her own. How do you buy five uniforms? Find lunch money for five children? Five bus passes? Little things like that. I'm making money, but Mum was working every hour God sent at St Ann's Hospital, in the physiotherapy department. That's not a rapper's wage! She had to make some really difficult choices. So if there was a school trip, she had to decide who could go. All five of us couldn't go to Thorpe Park. I don't even know how you get your head around those kinds of decisions. I can imagine how my mum must have felt when she saw everyone going on holiday. But how are you going to take five children on holiday? At half-term, when they put the prices up? Where are you going to go? The pressure never let up on her. I wonder if the only reason she coped is because she knew she didn't have the luxury of cracking. There was no Parent B to step in and take over.

My son went to play out for the first time not long ago, and I texted, 'Mum, I'm sorry. I get it.' You can't describe the feeling. You tell him to be back by 7 p.m., it's 6 p.m. and you're already freaking out. You're anxious, you're waiting for something to happen, even though you know it probably won't. I even tweeted about it, and Giggs messaged me back: 'Bro! I'm actually driving around right this minute looking for my kid!' All the hype about being a rapper, being cool and unflappable, just evaporates when it's five minutes after curfew and your child's not home. I realised why my mum would shout at me if I got home ten minutes late, or if my phone died and she couldn't call me. I was seeing the other side of the coin. The head was appreciating the tails for once. My mum was a smacker. With her, it was always like, 'You know the boundary. Do not even approach it.' That's what I take from her, because kids are always pushing. But even they know there's a level that they can get to, and they know what's going to happen if they get there – then they understand.

When I speak to my mum about it now, she's always like, 'I wasn't that bad!' But I see it from her perspective now. You're tired and stressed. You've wrestled to get in the bathroom. You've gone to work. You've come home. The house isn't tidy. The food isn't cooked. The drink that you're working to buy is finished. Just little dumb things. Like someone has put the emergency credit on the electric, but hasn't said. So the next time it runs out we have to go to the shop, or have to go and find a shop, regardless of what time it is. It's little things like that. It must be hard. Some mornings we'd get up and knock on her door: 'Mum, you got the bus pass money?' And you might not get an answer. Those days when I'd do something at school, and I'd be waiting for her to go nuts when I got home, only for her to just shake her head and say, 'I can't deal with this today.' At the time I thought that was a result! Now, I realise her silence was worse than her blowing up.

Just put yourself in her position for a second. You've gone to work, you're going through hell, and there's nothing coming back for you. I understand it now. She must have been so tired and stressed. Especially as all that work, all the hours you're putting in, still means you're only just getting by. It's not even like at the end of the month she could say, 'Right, I'm going to Jamaica.'

It's hand to mouth. Christmas was cancelled every other year, birthday presents were a card and then something at the end of the month on payday. Her whole life was on IOU. The temptation to just walk out the door and not come back must've been there, on some level. But she didn't have the option. Or at least, she never acted like she had the option. In my eyes, that's the definition of strength.

I hope my mum knows I understand what she did for us. We've talked about it a few times, here and there, but I don't think I've ever set it out as concretely as I've done here. I suppose it's impossible to match her sacrifice with a gesture of my own. I can only try. I can't treat her to anything. I bought her a watch not long ago, and she said, 'Oh, that's nice. I'll wear it when I go out.' But she never goes out! It's just going to sit in the box. My mum doesn't ever want to go out. I can book a restaurant for us, and just before we're supposed to go she'll call and say, 'Have you paid for it?' and I'll say no. 'So let's not go. It's going to be too expensive.' I've realised that she just likes what she likes. She's a creature of habit. So instead of going out to a restaurant, we'll pick up a takeaway and go to her house. It's what she prefers. The time with us is what matters. So we go to her house a lot, for games night and that sort of thing. That is, for her, a holiday. We play a lot of Articulate! and me and my sister just go to war. No mercy, no loyalty. Our family put us on different teams just to see us go at it. I won't lie, I win a lot. I'm not the smartest, but I'm more strategic. Maybe my next book will be on Articulate! tactics.

So I'll use this song to explain exactly how I feel about my mum, and how I get that across in music. Because writing, whether on a track or in print, is how you set something down as history. And if it's important enough, or resonates with enough people, maybe one day that history will become a legend. That's why in 'Mummy's Boy' I use *allusion* – a reference to Ancient Greek myth:

> Well, he's gone and built a house
> Guess I'm Hercules
> World view, call my mama 'Zeus'
> 'Cause she's worthy

If I'm the hero, she's the deity. It's a way of playing with gender expectations as well. I could've portrayed my mum as a domestic goddess, and talked about how much I appreciate all the cooking and cleaning. But that keeps her trapped in a little box. It says that her only worth as a woman comes from doing typically feminine things. I wanted to show that she didn't just keep a house, she carried the whole thing on her shoulders. The good qualities that me and my sisters have ('When

I look in the mirror I see my mummy, boy / All my four different sisters look like my mummy, boy') are reflections of the virtues that she embodies. My work ethic comes from her ('See now I work for a living 'cause of my mummy, boy / 'Cause she was handling business when I was unemployed') – and it was that moral nourishment, as well as food on the table, that had us growing up healthy ('It's like she stirred courage in that corn beef pot'). There's no way I could have been the father I am without having been a mummy's boy first.

In life you don't give to receive. There's no celebration for being a good parent, there's no certificate. You can only gauge how well you've done by how well your children have done. My mum asks a lot, 'Was I a good mum?' How am I meant to answer that? We grew up on one of the roughest estates in Tottenham. We went through some difficult times. But we're all doing OK. We're doing well. What more do you want? It's something I still see with my children's mother, and with my partner. The pressures are immense on women to raise their kids right. Because society is constructed so that men can always walk away. Women don't really have that option, and they'll always get the blame if things go wrong. There's always insecurity. Am I doing the right thing? There's love, there's care, there's a roof and there's food. That's what you build from, everything else is a bonus. You don't need to care about anything else.

There's no one specific person I go to for advice on parenting. A few of my bredrins had kids before I did. When I knew I was going to be a father, my first questions were, is it expensive? How much money will I need? Stupid questions. Little did I know that was the easy stuff. There are so many other concerns when you're parenting children, because it's not like you're raising a litter of cubs and you've just got to keep them alive through the dry season. You're responsible for how they turn out as people. For their moral development, their character. You can always borrow money, but you can't borrow integrity.

I see myself in both of them. My son is quiet, calm, in his own head a lot of the time, like me. He looks like butter wouldn't melt, but I'm pretty sure it's melting! I remember speaking to my uncle Stafford just after we found out we were having a boy. He said that raising boys was harder than raising girls. You want the boy to be a man, so you show him love, but you want him to be independent. You will watch him fall over, and want to pick him up, but feel like you have to leave him to get back up by himself. And to get him thinking that he can do it, that he doesn't have to rely on you. That's hard when all you want to do as a parent is keep him safe.

I want to show him that being strong as a man doesn't mean denying your emotions or being cold. But at the same time, I want to make sure he's resilient enough to cope with everything the world's gonna throw at him. How do you know the difference between too tough and tough enough when it comes to raising boys? It's harder being a man raising a boy, because you want him to have all your virtues and none of your flaws – and then also protect him from the experiences that'll teach him which are which! I didn't believe Stafford at first, but as usual, time proved him right.

My daughter is adventurous. She also remembers everything, and she won't take any nonsense. Her school will call up and say she's in trouble for shouting at a boy in her class, and when I ask her about it she'll talk me through what happened, step by step: 'On Tuesday he was pushing me, and I told the teacher. On Thursday he pushed me again. On Friday he didn't do anything, but today he pushed me again. So I shouted at him.' You can't argue with her, because she has it all down. It's the same thing that I do. I see it completely. She's going to do something interesting one day.

The ambition I have for her is undercut by a certain sense of fear. Because I know that society's constructed to tear down women's self-esteem. I work in an industry that builds girls up just to watch them fall. I measure the hopes I have for my daughter against the pressures

I know she'll be under. That's why I make an effort to tell her how special she is. This is a strategy I talk about in 'Mummy's Boy' as well:

> *I tell her she's important 'cause she's daddy's girl*
> *I'll hold you together in this shattered world*
> *Social media won't affect you like the man himself*

It's a similar sentiment to the *Black Mirror* reference in 'Upon Reflection', but here I'm positioning real-life ties as a counterweight to all the bile and hate on social media. I want to be an anchor for her in the real world, so she never loses her way online.

In '6 Words', I represent parental love as being just as blissful and ecstatic as romance. But in 'Mummy's Boy', even though I'm talking about parent–child bonds again, I'm showing the love in a different light. There are two moments when I explore this in depth. The first is when I talk about the feeling of helplessness I experienced when my daughter was in hospital ('Think I gave a fuck about opp / When my daughter had an op / Had a feeling in my heart / But if she needs it, then I'd swap in a second'). The second is talking about how, even though I drove my mum up the wall with some of my mischief, like borrowing her car and getting chased by police, still she 'tried to defend me, rather they put cuffs on' her.

In both these parts, I'm characterising love as something sacrificial. The bond between parent and child isn't only about you having given them life – it's so strong that you would give up your life to save theirs. In Ancient Greek, the word for this is *agape*. That feeling of being willing to give up your life as proof of your love runs very deep in our culture. 'Agape' is used in the Bible to describe the love God has for his creation, and the sacrifice of his son for the eternal life of man. And in return, the same word is used to describe the love of man for God. So in 'Mummy's Boy', I reciprocate my mum's willingness to give up her freedom for me: 'Probably do life twice over to see I'm comfortable / Swear I'd give my life twice over to give you life support'. It's a theme which links back to that Hercules/Zeus imagery – the bond between parent and child, between deity and creation.

Becoming a parent marks the moment you clock that your life doesn't belong to you. It's like your heart's been given up in a transplant, and you can feel it running around in a new body that's falling over and scraping its knee all the time. You're in thrall to a love that's so strong, you would give up your own survival in a second in order for this life you've produced to keep growing. It makes you realise that half the struggle of being a parent is coming to terms with your own fragility. All your ego and all your boasting goes out the window: the first time you hold your baby, you know for a fact that this tiny person, who can't even lift up their own head, has got you wrapped around their little finger. You're reckoning with your own loss of control, right at the moment you mature into the man you were always meant to be.

I wouldn't be the songwriter I am without that perspective.

6.

THE JUSTICE
('OPEN CONVERSATION &
MARK DUGGAN')

> And then the justice,
> In fair round belly with good capon lin'd,
> With eyes severe and beard of formal cut,
> Full of wise saws and modern instances;
> And so he plays his part.

If they shoot me down, would you riot for me?

Open Conversation & Mark Duggan

Grown on me
Can't sing but I wrote you a song that's grown on me
And my treasures have grown on me
Aware of the responsibilities, grown on me
And when I wear a suit and tie, it looks grown on me
I ain't changed, I'm just a new old me
Or did you know me?
Grown on me

(Music so gorgeous, got you feeling flawless)
(Music so gorgeous, got you feeling flawless)
(Mu-mu-music so gorgeous, got you feeling flawless)
(Music so gorgeous, got you feeling flawless)
(Music so gorgeous, got-got you feeling flawless)

Uh, I grew up on Eternal, I'm tryna be the same
Ever seen a flame in the rain?
No? Then you've never seen Jermaine
In his white-gold chain back in the day, just give me space
Yeah
Though I might have took a Galaxy
I never had a pound
Couldn't afford a Ford so I had to run around
What the fuck's an allergy?
All my niggas nuts
We weren't allowed in the youth club
Before we hit the clubs
They said enough was enough
So we had to give 'em more
When you see sides, I just wanna know you're sure
Are you sure?
Or do you sympathise?
You grew up on Kinder Surprise
I had licks and rice and had to drink my pride
One-on-one since six or five
Lost my marbles, looking down the drain
Tryna find 'em, I couldn't find 'em
(Look a little closer to home, you might find 'em)
I might find 'em?
Fuck that, I've got my skateboard
I've got my rucksack, I've got my eight balls
I've got two sticks and I ain't playing pool

I know who's who, I'm from the same school
And it's hard knocks, where it makes you
Or it breaks you, I didn't snap in half
I just snapped in class
It's a miracle I didn't catch that charge
Ain't got time to waste
Night time, that's like my time of day
When you're 32 shades of grey
In this concrete jungle, you've gotta pave a way
Just don't let 'em take your Jane
(Can't take you, baby)
I start playing Jason when they get adjacent
You know how that movie goes
Click-clack, bang-bang on my foes, 2Pac taught me that
Biggie Smalls taught me swag
Got my Versace shirt, put my car in reverse
I was hypnotised with Medusa in my lenses
Now I'm Medusa to my exes
Don't look at me, don't look at me
Unless you've got the whole booking fee
I used to have a hole in my jeans
Holes in my tee
Now I buy outfits for the whole of my team
You couldn't shot on the block I live
Moving Bobby Brown, that was just my prerogative
Just my prerogative
Driving cars with no indicators

I took a right turn with no indication
The only stimulation was ipi-dipi-dation
How many of my niggas am I seeing in the station?
I'm getting fed up
Remember they put the cuffs on me
Felt like I couldn't even stand up or breathe
Brother Mark never made it to custody
I see his kids now and again
I give them every cent that I've got up in my pocket
But it isn't enough
'Cause when he saw me at the lights, he said give me
    your number
Got the same school shirt, now I'm wearing
    this jumper
Saying RIP
Just know you R-I me
Every verse from your coffin and I'm not stopping
See the pressures we had, tryna take it off them
Turned the hangman rope into straight white gold
Cuh we rose from the dungeon
Zeros to the hundreds
And they can write books on us where we come from
That's why we're heroes on our junction

Grown on me
Can't sing but I wrote you a song that's grown on me
And my treasures have grown on me

Aware of the responsibilities, grown on me
And when I wear a suit and tie, it looks grown on me
I ain't changed, I'm just a new old me
Or did you know me?
Grown on me

(Music so gorgeous, got you feeling flawless)
(Music so gorgeous, got you feeling flawless)
(Mu-mu-music so gorgeous, got you feeling flawless)
(Music so gorgeous, got you feeling flawless)
(Music so gorgeous, got-got you feeling flawless)

Who are the murderers?
Police are the murderers!
No justice? No peace!
No justice? No peace!
No justice? No peace!
We don't do this because we want to do this
We don't do this because we read in a book that it's a
    good thing to do
We do this because for generations, they've been
    killing black people all over the country
Poor and working-class people all over the country
And always getting away with it

I heard it's all been love
Cupid, draw back your bow

We need to follow that arrow
While I'm on my feet
If they shoot me down, would you riot for me?
Riot for me
We need to follow that arrow
As long as we believe
Two tears falling like the innocent
Spirits in the wind
What's respect if they expect silence?
Oh
Sirens when we disrespect
Sirens when we disrespect
What's respect if they expect silence?
We hear sirens when we disrespect, yeah

I just lost my mind
I just lost my mind
Is it me or am I scared of the cops outside?
There's cops outside
There's an I in team but I'm on my side, I guess
Roses are red
Violets for the violence
Yeah

What's respect if they expect silence?
We hear sirens when we disrespect

I was born in 1985 in Tottenham, the same year as the riots. A woman called Cynthia Jarrett had died after police raided her house, and just the week before another woman called Cherry Groce had been shot by the police in Brixton. It all kicked off on the estate – there were demonstrations and protests, fires, and a policeman was killed. My dad and grandparents had their house raided: I was barely a newborn, but had experienced my first riot. I remember going to visit an uncle in prison when I was eighteen years old, and meeting Winston Silcott. It was weird knowing he'd been in jail for my whole life. You've got to understand that where I'm from, you grow up on the wisdom of your elders. Their experience of how society treated them shapes how you view the world. History isn't something which stays in the past.

There are some things so terrible that they cast a shadow over your whole life. Not just your future, but how you remember things. Mark Duggan's death is one of those things for me. When I heard what had happened to him, and saw the riots unfold across Tottenham and the rest of the country, it was like everything had shattered. When you're trying to make sense of something so chaotic, you start looking for signs in your past that it was always going to happen. Wretchrospect makes the impossible look like the inevitable. That's how I ended up writing a song like 'Open Conversation & Mark Duggan' – it's a meditation on all those little patterns that you identify in hindsight.

That day in the studio, Mo was just messing around on the piano. We'd taken a break and then I heard those soft chords – G flat major drifting into B flat minor, D flat major, E flat major over G, E flat minor over G flat, E flat minor, looping back again – and I stopped him in his tracks. 'What song is this?'

'Nothing, I'm just messing.'

Something about that melancholy chord progression touched me deeply – and suddenly I knew what I had to write a song about.

Normally I'm afraid of gaps in songs. I like to use up every single millisecond in a bar. I'll write down the entire length of the page so that absolutely nothing is left unsaid. But it was the spaces in Mo's piano composition which made it beautiful to my ear. In art, this is known as *negative space*: the idea that you see an object through the emptiness around it. And because this song is remembering Mark Duggan, and what the events of 2011 meant for the community and his friends and family, I thought this approach was a fitting memorial. His name hangs over the song as the title, but it takes you nearly three minutes before you hear me say it out loud. This is a song that's written from the void. The whole point of an elegy – a lament for the dead – is that you're left reflecting in the space left behind by the person who passed away.

In 2011, looking around at the aftermath of the riots, everything just felt too close. A family was grieving, Tottenham was grieving, and I didn't want to be just another talking head taking advantage of a tragedy in order to make a name for themselves. Lots of people at the time wrote songs about the riots, and while they could give a sense of the anger, they couldn't convey the sadness. I mean, most of the time you were listening to songs written from the perspective of people watching the news. The job of a songwriter and the job of a commentator are two different things. You need to see what it is you don't know, and own it. And be confident. Friends of mine get very frustrated simply because certain people aren't speaking out about particular issues. But you can only speak about what you know. In this age of social media, artists are under so much pressure to have a view on everything. Why? And then Giggs takes Piers Morgan to task about something he's said on Twitter, and everyone criticises Giggs for the way he expresses himself. What did you expect? He's being honest. Silence is taken to mean you don't care.

Because you feel so responsible, when things are thrown onto you. It's daunting. But you need to remember that the people who are asking for opinions don't even care about the subject matter. With a lot of journalists, their intentions are not pure. It's entertainment. All that's going on in their mind is 'if it bleeds, it leads'. It's turning someone's life and death into a spectacle. There's no honour in it. Who's going to learn anything from that?

It took five years for me to feel ready to speak on Mark publicly. To feel like I'd grown into the gravity of the task. So I start the song reflecting on where I am in my career:

> Grown on me
> Can't sing but I wrote you a song that's grown on me
> And my treasures have grown on me
> Aware of the responsibilities, grown on me
> And when I wear a suit and tie, it looks grown on me
> I ain't changed, I'm just a new old me

I wanted 'Open Conversation & Mark Duggan' to read like two pages from a diary. I'm not explaining myself to the listener, I'm talking to myself. I'm looking at where I am now, and looking back to think about everything that's changed in the past few years. I've grown into a new fabric. In every sense, what I'm wearing now fits me better than the suit Mum forced me into, two sizes too big. If I saw someone wearing a suit fifteen years ago, my first thought would be were they going to court or something. It's not like anyone we know is getting married, so it's definitely not a wedding. And from our neighbourhood, it's probably not a job interview either. But time passes, things change, then one day the suit stops wearing *you*, and you start wearing it. But it's not all about dressing sharp. With success and growth come responsibilities. You don't just wear a suit at Fashion Week; it's what you wear for a funeral too.

I'm trying to tell you that I grew up on that naughty side of town. I'm not coming from Barnet, I'm coming from Tiverton Estate in Tottenham. I've got to take you back to when I was that young Wretch on the ends:

Uh, I grew up on Eternal, I'm tryna be the same
Ever seen a flame in the rain?
No? Then you've never seen Jermaine
In his white-gold chain back in the day, just give me space

The imagery here of the 'flame in the rain' is saying that I knew I had that spark even when I was listening to my sister's R&B records. When I was in my white-gold chain days, you'd look at my smile and think that butter wouldn't melt, but these times it was full-on evaporating! I was a real little wretch. And that sense of mischief is something I carry through in the next bars:

> *Yeah*
> *Though I might have took a Galaxy*
> *I never had a pound*
> *Couldn't afford a Ford so I had to run around*

There's a lot in these lines. On the surface, it's just talking about those days when I'd nick a chocolate bar from the shop because I was short of P; I wasn't making enough money to be able to drive so I was walking about on foot.

But read those bars again: the same way 'Eternal' connects across to the next line with 'flame', here you're supposed to put 'Galaxy' and 'Ford' together. A Ford Galaxy was the make of the taxi that Mark was travelling in the day he was taken. Using imagery in this way – where you take something out of chronological order and use it earlier in the narrative – is a form of *prolepsis*. Prolepsis is normally defined as foreshadowing: you use it to hint at what's coming next in the story. Sometimes foreshadowing is used by authors who want to build up suspense, or let the reader in on a plot that the characters don't yet know about.

But in 'Open Conversation & Mark Duggan' I'm using prolepsis a bit differently. Imagine a stained-glass window in a church, one that depicts the life and martyrdom of a saint. Your eyes trace the multicoloured patchwork, and you piece together a story from the panels. Now imagine that the stained-glass window has been smashed with such force from the inside outwards that its shards scatter everywhere. Not just around the grounds of the churchyard, but over the surrounding streets and roundabouts and front gardens. For months, people keep finding jagged pieces of rose, blue and gold on the pavement. Maybe one day in a pile of autumn leaves, you come across the fragment of a face you half recognise. That's what my version of prolepsis is, except instead of fragments scattering across space, they're scattering across time. It's like the shots that took Mark away blasted apart his whole life story, and I keep finding pieces of it embedded in my memories. So going back to 'I might have took a Galaxy', this little hint of Mark makes you see that bar in a whole new light. It's got the beginning of my life and the end of his. You start thinking about how some crimes, like stealing a chocolate bar, get you a slap on the wrist. Others – even if nothing's proved in court – get you a death penalty.

Musing on the Galaxy sets off a whole chain of reminiscing. The next sixteen-bar puts you back in my shoes as a kid going to youth clubs. There were a few of us – some hyperactive yutes testing boundaries ('What the fuck's an allergy? / All my niggas nuts'). We were forever acting up and being threatened with being kicked out. There were always those youth workers trying to assert themselves, and it would just make us push back harder: 'They said enough was enough / So we had to give 'em more'. Are you disciplining us because you actually sympathise with our situation, or do you just want to prove that you can win a battle of wills against a bunch of mischievous yutes? Are you going to send us out, or are you actually trying to send a message? Either way, we're gonna flip. Heads we win, tails you lose.

Sometimes the people sent to deal with us simply couldn't relate. They had grown up with ideal childhoods ('You grew up on Kinder Surprise'), whereas for us there were higher stakes and different rules that came with them ('I had licks and rice and had to drink my pride / One-on-one since six or five'). We were born into conflict, and our parents had to raise us tough enough to survive it. That can be very harsh. Our upbringing was based on tough love, and I can see why. It's not cuddles, or 'I love yous'. I was never bullied, but if I had been, I would have had no idea who to turn to. My mum would have said, 'What do you mean, you're

being bullied? But you're in here running your mouth . . .'
and so on. No one ever said, 'How are you feeling?' We
never dealt with our issues. We just moved on to the
next thing. Nothing was ever resolved.

So that kid you're going toe-to-toe with in the youth
club or the classroom – is he going nuts, or is he lost?
You can look at someone acting up as a challenge to your
authority, or you can look at it as a way of reaching out.

> Lost my marbles, looking down the drain
> Tryna find 'em, I couldn't find 'em
> (Look a little closer to home, you might find 'em)
> I might find 'em?

Here, I'm trying to convey a sense of the innocence I had,
but that others didn't recognise in me until it was gone.
This is a kid's cry for help.

If the youth club won't have you, then the streets will
take you. You start by kicking back and walking out
('Fuck that, I've got my skateboard') and then you
quickly realise you've got to stand on your own two feet.
So what have I got to be able to support myself? It's the
ghetto repertoire: 'I've got my rucksack, I've got my
eight balls / I've got two sticks and I ain't playing pool'.
Once more, images that should be playful are undercut
by a dark meaning. Sticks and eight balls are double
entendres. On the surface level, they're obviously

referring to the equipment you need to play pool. But if you're familiar with the slang, you'll pick up that I'm talking about guns and drugs. There's something else in here too, though, a little glimmer of hope which gives you a clue to why I didn't get trapped in that life. When I was growing up, you'd either be the boy with the skateboard or BMX, or you'd be the one with the rucksack and the rollerblades, artistic and into backpack rap. I was a bit of both – and it's that combination which makes me the writer I am.

I won't shy away from it: I could be a proper handful as a yute. The line between the streets and the classroom was very blurred ('I know who's who, I'm from the same school'), so it was like I was getting two kinds of education at once. Some people can't take that kind of pressure, but my instinct was always to break the system before it broke me. So 'I didn't snap in half / I just snapped in class' – I'll put myself on the front foot and attack, rather than let myself be taken down by all the people looking at me with hatred, fear or suspicion. I'm the breaker, I'm the disrupter. And I'm not going to be swallowed up by all the forces out to make me fail. But looking back on it, that response carried its own risks. 'It's a miracle I didn't catch that charge' – losing my temper in class could have seen me waste a lot more time than just sitting in detention, if you know what I mean. It was a *Sliding Doors* kind of moment. Had things gone the other way, I could have spent the rest of my youth locked up in prison, forever criminalised even when I got out. I could have just as easily been in Mark's position later on in life.

Because for a time I was swerving around, directionless ('Driving cars with no indicators / I took a right turn with no indication'). It's a bit like Al Capone getting done for tax evasion – I got caught over a petty crime, but not the thing I was actually doing. I wasn't alone in that experience. 'How many of my niggas I'll be seeing in the station? / I'm getting fed up' – being pursued by police, and feeling the full brutal force of them, was part of all our lives back then, and it was exhausting. Like in-the-marrow-of-your-bones exhausting. You might argue that it's hypocritical to complain about how police treat you if you're breaking the law, but think about it: if you're from a certain background, you're systematically excluded from all the things that help keep you on the straight and narrow. You're kicked out of class for the slightest thing; you can't get a good job because of the colour of your skin. You're surrounded by people who are forced to break the law just to get enough to survive. And more than that, regardless of what you actually do, you're automatically assumed to be involved in criminal activity because of where you live. So many people end up behind bars for something they didn't do.

Not everyone gets punished the same way for the same crime. Evidence shows that from stop and search to sentencing, the system is more likely to treat you harshly if you're a black man. I've been on the receiving end of that. I remember when 'they put the cuffs on me / Felt like I couldn't even stand up or breathe'. And that feeling of suffocation isn't even the worst of it. It's the lack of control. You're not the author of how this story ends: your life is in the hands of the officers arresting you. In this country you're meant to have rights, you're meant to be treated fairly. We don't have capital punishment. But 'Brother Mark never made it to custody' – the death penalty exists here for certain kinds of people on the wrong day. When you're pulled over by the police, you can feel it. They *want* to put the cuffs on you. They *want* a reason to use that taser or that gun. There's this barely concealed mania you can detect, as though deep down they're like, 'I've been training for fifteen years to use this, I've been practising on fake targets with blanks – and now I've got the real thing. You just fucking blink, mate.' The mad thing in those situations is that they're not clear on what they're saying. So you're not clear on what to do. One's screaming 'Stand up!', one's shouting 'Hands up!' and one's going 'Hands by your side!' It's chaotic.

*

Throughout the song, Mark is like a spirit. You feel his presence, even if you can't see him directly. I'm caught in the strange position of knowing the person who's being used as the cautionary tale by everyone else. For other people, he's like a myth or something. You might identify with him, you might even empathise, but there's still a lot of distance there. It's a theory to you, like in science when you learn about what happens when you mix acid and alkali. But for me it's the practical. He wasn't 'Mark Duggan' to me, he was just Brother Mark. He was a friend. At the time he was killed, I was approached for interviews constantly. My label pushed me to talk publicly too. What these journalists didn't understand is that what was a news clipping to them was a real person to me. I know the family and what they're going through, I know his kids. How could I be capable of sitting down and having a filmed conversation about it? I found it so distasteful even to consider the idea that I'd be up on *London Tonight* talking about it, just when my album happens to be out, looking like I'm taking advantage. And there were people who'd go on TV just to say awful things, racist things, to stir up controversy and keep themselves in media appearances for the next few years. I wanted no part of it. That's why I shunned the whole thing. It's disgusting that the media would expect someone close to the person who's been killed to treat the whole thing like a conversation piece. Why would you even want that? A man's life shouldn't be up for debate.

During the riots it felt like being at the eye of a storm. It was as if Mark's life being taken created this hole, and around it was a swirl of chaos just getting bigger and bigger. I felt weirdly separated from a lot of what was going on, while at the same time being jolted by seeing my neighbourhood in flames. When it's your story, the rioting doesn't feel like *Ill Manors*, as good as that was. When you're at the centre of it, everything just feels surreal.

That's another reason why I wouldn't have been able to answer the questions the media would have put to me at the time. Everyone would have been asking some version of 'Do you condone the rioting?' At the time, I probably would have snapped and said, 'Yeah, I fucking do!' Because the man who died was my friend, and I'd want to respond out of anger. I felt enraged at the idea that he could be killed without anyone making a noise about it. It's like leaving someone to die in the dark. But when you have responsibility, and you have young fans who look up to you and respect your opinion, you have to speak more thoughtfully. I was worried about encouraging anyone who was on the fence about taking part.

Now obviously I won't defend destroying people's homes, or independent businesses. I remember when

Allied Carpets got set on fire, and a house nearby ended up ablaze as well. A woman was in there, trapped on the top floor with a baby in her arms, and some local people had to rescue them both. It's good that in the midst of all that violence and fuckery, there's still a heart in the community. But it shouldn't have had to happen in the first place. I can't stand up and applaud a woman and a baby being frightened for their lives. But I also can't help but wonder: if there wasn't an uproar, how many more times would the police be able to kill with impunity? When you rob someone of their life through violence, what can you expect but more violence? Leaping to condone or condemn the consequences of Mark's death means that you miss the opportunity for understanding. It's like trying to condemn a hurricane. Berate it all you want, but you won't stop it in its tracks or prevent the next one from happening.

With 'Open Conversation & Mark Duggan', the whole point of the song is to humanise the kinds of people the media tell you to demonise. That's why the first time you hear his name in the song, you hear 'Brother Mark'. It's not the name you're used to hearing – the myth, the criminal, the riot guy. This is a different version of a story you think you already know. After the reference to not making it to custody, my focus shifts to the aftermath of his killing. You won't get the gory details of the shooting from me. What I'm writing comes from a place of real tenderness and affection. There's a lot of my own survivor's guilt woven into the lines 'I see his kids now and again / I give them every cent that I've got up in my pocket / But it isn't enough'. I'm already Uncle to every yute in the ends. But when I see Mark's kids playing, it's as though everything else fades away into the background and they're the only kids I can see. Because I know the trauma they've been through. The word 'sympathy' is inadequate to describe what I feel seeing them. What can you give them, to compensate for the loss they've experienced? Nothing is enough. Nothing can replace a father.

Mark's kids went through two losses. The first was their dad being taken from them when he was a young man himself. The second was what the media and the politicians did to tarnish his memory. Back in 2011, when the police realised just how much they'd fucked up, stories started getting leaked to the press. All that stuff, which later got disproven, about how Mark was firing a gun back at them and bullets got lodged in a police radio. They couldn't just put their hands up and admit they'd made a mistake. Think about it: as a parent, one of the first things you teach your children is that it's OK to make mistakes, as long as you own up and don't try to cover it up. And the most powerful people in the country couldn't live up to that very basic standard. No wonder people don't trust the police where I'm from – you're trying to tell us Mark somehow managed to throw a gun, in a way that witnesses didn't see, while he was being shot at the same time. You expect us to believe that? There was so much coming out about Mark in the immediate aftermath of his death which was just downright implausible. I remember reading how he was one of the top twenty-five most dangerous gangsters in Europe. Who the fuck made that list up? Where did that come from?

It was like the police were trying to unpaint a picture – to take an image of a man who we knew, and make him unrecognisable. It's as though they were taking a pen to a drawing of a star, separating all the lines out, and turning it into a swastika. All these untruths served a purpose: it was to say that you shouldn't mourn this man who was shot in highly suspicious circumstances. Don't ask too many questions, because he deserved to die. Imagine how that must have felt for his children. That's why I wanted to write this song, so they've got someone sharing nice memories of their dad as well as all the horrible things that've been said in the press. God only knows what they've been told by the media, or heard from teachers. But at least they'll have this, from someone who was Uncle to them even before Mark passed away. As a parent, you want to make sure these kids have something about their father that they can really trust.

More personally, it's something I also needed in order to process what happened. To make sense of the senseless. Whenever you get that call telling you someone's passed away, the first thing you do is think about the last time you saw them. When I found out what happened to Mark, my mind went right back to when he'd bumped into me by Tottenham Hale: ''Cause when he saw me at the lights, he said give me your number'. We spoke like the traffic lights hadn't just turned green – 'Rah, what's going on with you, you good?', that kind of thing – and an intention to keep in touch. Just a very normal, human connection. When people hear about Mark, they want the most sensational story possible – either a saint or a serial killer. But that's not who he was to us. That's why I focus on the little things, like that chance encounter or the fact we both went to Northumberland Park. We grew up in the same ends, we went raving at the same nightclubs. Mark was a couple of years older than me. When I was in Year 7, he was in Year 10 – which feels like an absolute lifetime at that age! When I think of how Mark was at school, it's completely at odds with how the media presented him later. You could tell he had two sides. And the ladies loved him, that always remained the same.

It's so strange that a day comes when you get older than your olders. But in another way, I feel like Mark never stopped ageing. Like there's a parallel timeline for him which just kept going. I won't ever delete Mark's number. It sounds crazy, but I feel like he's there – just not *here*. I think I get that way of thinking from my dad – he won't ever throw away a pair of shoes that he's worn to bury someone in, so I won't either. In a way it's horrid to think that as I get older, my closet is just going to get more and more filled by those muddy shoes. In art, they used to have this idea of a *memento mori* – a little reminder in every work that death is everywhere, and it comes for everyone. So you could have a picture of a lavish party, with food and drink and dancing, but in one corner there'll be a skull to cast a shadow over the whole scene. I suppose that's what the shoe thing is about. Every morning I open my wardrobe, and I'm reminded that you have to learn to live with death.

This sentiment is only as depressing as you want it to be. The duality of youth and untimely death are closely twinned together, for obvious reason, in 'Open Conversation & Mark Duggan':

> Got the same school shirt, now I'm wearing this jumper
> Saying RIP
> Just know you R-I me

Maybe if it was a different kind of song, that line would have been 'Grew up in the same hood, now I'm wearing this jumper'. But I had to make it more personal, and load it with memory. So on the one hand, there's more of that sense of dark foreshadowing in linking together our shared school shirt with the memorial jumper I'd wear after Mark's death. But on the other, the rest in peace/rest in me bar is meant to show that someone isn't truly gone if you keep their memory alive, if you share what you know about them and not just what you've heard. It's a privilege that as an artist I get to share memories of Mark with people.

Mark's death means I have a duty to make sure I don't waste a single second of my life: 'Every verse from your coffin and I'm not stopping'. This isn't a clichéd live-every-second-as-though-it's-your-last kind of thing. It's about doing right by Mark's children, and making sure they're OK. As Mark's friend, as a father myself, I've a responsibility to help guide those kids.

The next bar is pure alchemy: 'Turned the hangman rope into straight white gold'. My and Mark's generation inherited a curse. We were born with a noose around our necks that kept us comfortable on our own estate. But say the wrong thing, stray into the wrong ends, and you're finished. There was the whole Tottenham versus the surrounding boroughs thing, and we had no choice about it. You need to leave, but it's safer to stay. That's the pressure I'm trying to take off his children's shoulders. But just because those kids were born in a war doesn't mean they have to live in one. The 'straight white gold' line is taking you back to young Jermaine in his chain back in the day; I found wealth in what was around me, in what I had in me. Between those ingredients, I had what I needed to become a lyricist. This dungeon we were born into was also a cradle for art. There's power in knowing you can create out of tragedy. If necessity is the mother of invention, just think what survival can do. It's not good enough to be patted on the head just for trying – harsh circumstances mean you need to be putting out the very best of your work every time you make an attempt. Because we might be close to death every day, but we're capable of making something which is immortal.

Every single person where I'm from has a book in them. Not only the names you might have heard of, but the people you'd just walk past on a normal day. Everyone's had to survive and graft just to be here. That's what I meant when I said, 'And they can write books on us where we come from / That's why we're heroes on our junction': we make the history that historians are writing about. The people in power didn't deliver justice for Mark. MPs, journalists, talking heads – they all looked at an innocent man, whose life was taken without a trial or a guilty verdict, and all they saw was a statistic. One of the 'twenty-five most dangerous'. He was everything that was bad about Broadwater Farm, and nothing else. But that's not who he was to me. That's why I had to take extra care to shed light on all the positive things in his story, to push back against all the darkness that's been put on his name. This song is about removing all the ignorance that clouded the country's vision during the riots. I want you to see it as close to crystal clear as possible. My story for him is about human emotion: school, his kids, meeting at the traffic lights. And my story for me is about pushing boundaries, striving for excellence, and becoming the man who could tell this story right.

I grew up between two riots – 1985 and 2011 – but it's not those two events that define either Mark's life or mine. The ends we come from aren't just about violence and revenge. We're human. In 1988 a documentary was made about the estate called *Scenes from the Farm*, and there's a bit where you can hear my auntie and my uncle talk about what they want for me in life. My auntie, smiling and looking impossibly young, says she hopes I'll grow up into someone who 'we can all be proud of'; my uncle says he hopes that 'racism doesn't raise its head and avert my nephew, my godson, from getting what he deserves in life'.

Every parent nurtures certain hopes for their child. They work so that their young one can have a better life than they did. They want to see society change into something kinder. They don't want the obstacles that blocked their path to get in the way of their sons' and daughters'. And the world I grew up in is the sum total of all those elders' joys and tragedies, tribulations and successes. All those hopes. So what happens when you extinguish the life of someone's son at the point of a gun? You've taken away their hopes. You've stolen their future. It's no surprise there've been riots in Tottenham; what's surprising is that there haven't been more. People are pushed to the point of destruction when their basic human dignity isn't recognised by the people in power. It doesn't all come from a place of hate – they're motivated by love and loss too. That's why I'm asking: 'If they shoot me down, would you riot for me?'

7.

THE KING
('FIRE IN THE BOOTH PT 3', 'FIRE IN THE BOOTH PT 4', 'FIRE IN THE BOOTH PT 5')

Welcome to my humble abode, I live alone. Sticks and stones thrown at my bones, they never broke. While you was out following sheep, I killed a goat, I became the GOAT, had to take the throne.

We're on the home stretch now: Fire in the Booth, the pinnacle of my craft, where I'm the undisputed king. In my eyes, the king is a democrat at heart; the will of the people and the power he wields go crown-in-hand. He's not a tyrant ruling by divine right. He's the people's champ. And once he's in, they'll never vote leave. A true king isn't born into a monarchy. Instead, he's someone who builds his own palace brick by brick. A king commands respect by winning wars and vanquishing his enemies. The king is respected when he wins a war, but he's loved when he keeps the peace. Knowing how to do that means never losing sight of where you stand, who you represent and why their voices need uplifting in the first place. It's your talent that makes you eligible for leadership, but it's your demeanour that makes you worthy. This means conducting yourself with humility.

Someone wore the crown before you, and someone else will wear it after you. No reign lasts for ever, but your legacy might.

It's often said that 'Heavy lies the head that wears the crown'. Well, Shakespeare actually used the word 'uneasy' – I'd personally say 'unhinged' – but I'm not really here to split hairs. Instead, I want to pose a question: where do you create the space for vulnerability at the height of your success? If you're carrying the world on your shoulders, how are you meant to unburden yourself? After he's had to fight his way to the top, who does the king confess to?

The studio is my sanctuary, my therapy room, and the 1Xtra tower is my confessional booth. There's something about doing a Fire in the Booth – the simplicity of going back to basics, the amount of care I put into the freestyle, the fact I record in one take – which brings out my best work as a lyricist. There's nothing to hide behind. It puts me in my fullest zone creatively. It's not like doing a song for an album, and you're thinking about where it fits in terms of what the record as a whole needs. All you need to do is produce something authentic, and that demonstrates your growth as an artist since the last time you were on. Because it's one thing to write a freestyle that goes viral. But to do three or four, under that kind of pressure? Any striker can have a good season. But what separates a Ronaldo or a Messi from the rest of the pack is that they have many.

Fire in the Booth is one of the most rigorous tests for a rapper. I know that as soon as I step in there, I've got to be at the apex of my craft. Charlie Sloth knows just how to get me onto the show: he won't prod or pester, he'll just drop me a little message whenever someone else has done a sick freestyle. He knows how to activate my competitive streak! Because I can't settle for just being in the top five Fire in the Booths. Charlie knows I want to have the best one.

That's more of a healthy competition, though. I'm not looking to pull anyone down. Me getting in the booth is a recognition of the quality I see in other rappers. It takes a certain calibre of artist to make me step my game up. Avelino's Fire in the Booth was cold; Kano's been moving digital in there as well. Ghetts, of course, is right up there amongst the greats. They delivered excellence and left no room for others to doubt either their technical brilliance or their delivery. But for me the one that really stood out is when Jaykae did a freestyle after his friend Depz was killed. It was just so raw. Like, I don't know how much time he spent on writing the lyrics, but he made it sound as though he'd just found out about the tragedy, jumped in his car and released a storm into the mic. There was just so much power in his rage and in his grief. Watching it, you kind of felt the studio walls couldn't contain everything he was pouring out.

When you're doing a Fire in the Booth, it's not just for yourself. It's for the culture. Your work belongs to something bigger than you, because what you do on the battlefield will be memorialised in the museum that is the Internet. Every one of my Fire in the Booth performances is different. Each one narrates specific concerns I had at that time of my life, whether it's to do with my career, the world around me, or something traumatic I was trying to make sense of through music. But there are some similarities too: techniques that make an appearance in one, and then get developed in another.

Writing techniques shouldn't be thrown away after you use them once. They're meant to get better as time goes by, like fine wine ageing in a cellar. Or there are certain patterns of thought which come up again and again, because they're an integral part of who I am as a man. Rather than taking you through all my Fire in the Booths one by one, I've chosen the three which reflect me best as an artist: one I wrote shortly after Richard Antwi passed away ('pt 3'), one with Avelino which made a lot of noise ('pt 4'), and my most recent one to date ('pt 5'). I've chopped up the lyrics, selected the choicest cuts, and stitched them together in order to explore beginnings, middles and ends across all three freestyles.

Fire in the Booth pt 3

Not another nigga, nah, not another nigga

Dropped on the front line with a cop behind the trigger

Throw your spirit in the sky, probably drop you down and snigger

That's why every drop of Henny's like a shot inside my liver

Certain I'm the difference, but they'll probably beg to differ

Tryna spit my thousand words before they crop me out the picture

That a selfie, self-less, I'm self-raising

I had no P, outta breath, I kept chasing

Couldn't go sleep, no rest, this world's waiting on my Rolly

Hell yeah, you tell Satan that I pray to the Lord, pray to the
     most high

Penny for my thoughts, should get a monkey for most lines

I turned words into numbers

That made work for my brothers

From a kid in the bits to Columbus

Now the world's my circumference

My little man's talking 'bout bands, I just hope that my son's
     in the Mumfords

Hope he don't lose his way, the apple don't fall too far

The designer's the future in every way

And I'm better than Shakespeare, and I ain't writing any plays

Nor am I writing to get played, it's just my right to get the plays

I was underground 'cause it's alright to get the train

But if you was God's son would you be hiding in the shade?

I'm Rolling in the Deep, setting Fire to the Rain

And it's Written in the Stars in some Newton Oil Paint
When I craft my art, I favour Banksy
Man I'm Rich with life, I'm on my Antwi
You see I'll hold my weight until my hands bleed
Only got my word and my bars, swear on my canteen
Man if I punch lines, I'll show you hand speed
I will do a Strickland Banks before I Plan B
Nigga I go realer, you chimpanzee
Monkey I don't fancy dress, I dress fancy
You see I once was lonely to start off
Not now, these companies, I'm a part of
Verset that's that drink we own all of

I'll show you the flick of the wrist, because my arm's strong
Strength no weakness, doing press-ups like the kids
Now I'm trying to give my kids a head start
To get them set, on their marks
On this marathon of life I'm Gebrselassie, a son of Selassie I
Mo Farah, my brother, told me keep up my stride
More Stephen Lawrence than Boris, running to stay alive
Try crop me out picture like I'm Dame
But I'm just another Jigga with some glitter in my chain
Eight hundred on my frames, half a milli on my place
Only keep it 100 if I'm running with Usain
But I keep it 300 when I'm running with my mates
On some Louis Farrakhan, we ain't running from a race
I grew up in a maze, where I saw cats chasing their tails

Dogs selling to cats, man killing their dogs
The lost think that they're found, the found think that
    they're God
Fighting over ground, but to none of us it belongs
And the cons outweigh the pros, but the pros can weigh an oz
And turn coke into powder, that's just connecting the dots
Man, now are you tempted to shot?
Tempted to touch, attempted to murder
They tried to kill me before, nothing against me shall prosper
Money on my head, I'll have to Kevin my Costner
Coming for my bread, I'll turn your muscles to lobster
Wifey playing nurse, and guess who's playing the doctor?
Dr King, Dr Dre, man I sold pharmaceuticals, I did it the
    doctor way
I'm trying to meet Jay before he dashes the Roc away
'Cause Bishop show up prison, man, I'm only a block away
Rich said, 'Who wakes up and really wants to come second?'
Counting on my brother, got me counting all my blessings
Ever lost someone who found you with intentions on bringing
    something out of you to turn you to a legend?
When I heard the news I had to park up on the kerb
I was on the phone to Twin, and we didn't even say a word
I'm so used to pain, but there's a difference when it hurts
'Cause when they took away your body, man, it multiplied
    your worth, in my eyes
I had tears in my eyes, Dunn's River Fallin', man, I couldn't
    even dry cry

Spent time alone, see I just had to define life
The good die young, so your calling was primetime

Last time I came I competed with the world
Now this time I'm here I'm competing with myself
Don't put me in a bracket with no one, bro
I got so many bullet points, brother I overload
Add me to the magic you might give him an overdose
While I swim into a ocean, rock the boat, 'cause I overflow
I'm so used to splashing, man, I'm so used to splashing
Young Fire's on the rise, and he's just waiting for the baton
But I told him that he might have race me till I'm patterned
Got my master's in English, so I may resort to Latin
By the time you hear this, I'll be past gear six
And if they ain't dead already, they just had a near miss
I put the 'fear' in fearless
Pussy, get a smear test
And if it gets political, call me Tony Blair Witch
Why did we vote Leave? Why did we vote Leave?
The government's sending kids to sleep with no dreams
They're trying to tick a box, you would have thought they sold weed
Everybody's high, no wonder why the future's codeine
Codeine crazy, everybody dabbin', having codeine babies
Having March Madness, cause their Roley's 18
But I'm Mr Free B. A. Baracus, A-Team
With the top down, got the whip looking Page 3
Do you sympathise with me?

Started from the bottom, why they keep reminding me?
There's no similarities with you and I
If I gotta die to be the best, would you do or die with me?
I grew on the late Biggie hypnotising me
Am I grime? Am I rap? Why they keep dividing me?

Why they keep dividing me?
Everybody goes deep and can scuba-dive, yeah
They can all flow till they gotta synchronise with me
I made my own lane – can you see the drive in me?
I'm banned from every club – can you see the Nile in me?
There's hatred in my love – can you see the irony?
It's flamin' in my lungs – I should take this mic with me
'Cause I'm James Brown when he shot up the label
I'm Scarface with a key of coke on the table
Singing a song of praise, but I don't need no appraisal
'Cause I'm Pharrell Grindin', just tryna Pusha my ends
Spirit of DMX, singing Flesh of My Flesh
I'm Nas before Kelis and old school K. West – new school K. West
Still they all ain't Wretch
'Cause if they don't call me classic, gotta call me blessed
But I still do the sign of the cross, before I leave out
You can nail me to the cross – if you need now
If you keep calling me blood, and we don't bleed out, and let
    that shit run like rivers – you're in de-nial
Most Ws in the booth – I'm in the league now
This is called 'Fire in the Wretch' – 3-2 style

Fire in the Booth pt 4

Lately death's been getting ever so close

Been feeling spirits while I'm driving, I should get me a ghost

Growing up, didn't know the difference between the road and
    my home

Now I'm grown, I'm trying to buy every home on my road

Takeaway's been over-rinsed, I need a chef to come and
    live with me

Last time I picked up a pot, I nearly killed a fiend

I don't see a potent rapper out here that can mirror me

When I gave my kidneys to these kids, you must be
    kidding me

Do you remember playing Operation? (yeah)

That's how I feel about these compilations

Think they're the next Dr. Dre until they lose their patience

Saying the game's in a state, man, that's an understatement

I mean, how many more gems can I drop on the future?

How much of my fans just might not buy my new stuff?

We all got bars, but nobody here's a brewer

Bringing sandwich to the beach in the hope of finding tuna

This is nonsense – past tense

I'm a rap genius – I've passed sense

So if you ain't got a 2-1, or you ain't 3-2, you gotta graduate
    before you pass Wretch

We got off on the wrong foot because you half-step

Meanwhile, I'm getting restless because I can't rest

Twenty-one hours I'm awake, the other three I'm in a daze
  writing what to say with my last breath
Can you not hear the difference? Even when it's in your system?
Every time I flip the script, I got a scripture
I've seen man go from the strip to the strip club
I'm tryna go from eating Rich Tea to the rich club
I used to wanna go from the bits to the BRITs, cuz
And then I realised it's a fix when your skin's dark
Should I do a Kanye and keep it triller?
Fuck that, even when I lose, I'm the winner
I'm the people's champ, let me thank the people
Who never got the point until they grabbed the needle
Niggas tried to minus my pluses just to divide my people
Who go from stepping on roaches to stepping by The Beatles
It's progression at its finest
They say my weakness is kindness
I kill them with success, 'cause it's timeless
Every verse is a verse from the chapter of writing
The writing's on the wall, we know who Destiny's Child is
King Kendrick or Jermaine Cole
Or are you saying 'King Wretched' or 'Jermaine's Cold'?
I'm trying to lay the blueprint and give you reasonable doubt
So when you watch the throne, they can see me change clothes
Wait
You best believe that I'm a general
One of us has gotta compete at all the festivals
And I've been out here rapping for free before my testicles dropped

Man, I'm so credible, I'm incredible, uh
They say a promise is a comfort to a fool
I'm lying if I want to say I live in comfort, I'm the truth
And this will be the best Fire in the Booth
And I doubt they'll tell you different when I'm standing in
    the room
Why? Different class
Sometimes you have to ask:
'Do you want to be the best in your country or your school?'
In a country full of rules, where we're selling lollipop to
    keep them sucking on our balls
It's survival of the fittest, so I'm Mo Farah
I'm black as Akon, just tryna find my own Gaga
The less mercy you show could leave you merciless alone
But I'm yard grown, so I ain't talking no bad-up, nah
And Tidal's got the whole world moving crazy
It's like they rather a free Spotify playlist
That's messed up, like them cops on the day shift
Who just can't stop and search without tasing
Shit seems shocking when you're reading about it
Six years old they was raiding my house, shit
Tryna find my uncle, didn't open my mouth, shit
My dad mighta killed me – no snitching on our ship
The Titanic ain't going down because of me
See, I can't swim, but I'll be the anchor for the scene
See, how do they expect musicians to stay afloat
When all our sales keep going down the stream?

Fire in the Booth pt 5

Yes, 32 the album out right now
Love for the love
Fire in the Booth

Wrote this in the country, I was staring at horses
It's kinda nice to be still, I've been frankly detouring
I left my soul in every city, it's sad but it's honest
The amount of morning-after pills, I should have an
    endorsement
First year I really tapped into my audience
You won't be asked to pay respect if you cannot afford it
See, if the fruits of my labour's to rap every morning
I should Frank Ocean the label and channel my orange
I hope I'm one step away from that place there
They told us that Craig would only have seven days there
He came back, sky is just a limit we place there
Lightning struck twice, guess it really can rain here, I rate that
Water sign, yeah, I love the water splash and waves, fam
Used to want to be a Ninja Turtle when I was eight, fam
We were young shellers eating pizzas in estates, man
I'm still here in a tight circle, that's the same band
I pray I never see the day you're switching sides on me
We've always been adjacent, you could never slide off me
Now I'm living righteous, only fish in my body
Imma do or die properly, I got human rights on me

When your child dropped, it was like another child from me
And if it pops off, then we'll be side-by-side, obvy
I wish you all the best but that's never life's story
'Cause if Whitney was the moral, how would you define Bobby?
Think about it, and if you can't live without it
Don't let it go, take it home and build bricks around it
Just try to set it in stone, then stick around it
Any time you feel it in your soul, that's the gift about it
Disallow it or the control can make you drink about it
I fell in the zone and woke up in a liquor fountain
That's a tight space, a dark hole can have a thing about it
Bet you didn't know that going in could be a killer outing
I've had conversations with the best newcomers
And the worst old runners and the jewels they got were free
'Cause I can only give you me
They don't tell you how to live your dream without the sleep
How on the weekend you're the man but it gets lonely in
    the week
No surrender, no retreat, some family on your tree now
Can only see your branch when they used to hear your leaves
Used to share your feast
Then no one was hungry soon as the GOAT became
    the sheep
That's why I am pescatarian, it was sink or swim in the
    aquarium
Either break the glass or you share with them
Shots at me but I can only give what I receive

There's gunpowder on my clothes now, I'm washing
   my machine
I dealt with the matter when that was all that mattered
You ate all the pies while I was sharing out the platter
A Judas on the table is like a Buddhist with a hammer
Bringing peace with a piece, you want the passage or the passa?

Make your bed, you lie in it
I sleep so comfy, I hope I die in it
So if you wanna scar, lemme know, I'm lion king
I can make a movie, live for ever and die in it
They're praying on my downfall
So I took off in the spring and touched down in the fall
I hope I gave you what you wanted
Running from police, I was wanted
My future wasn't promised, that changed when my
   neighbours were the wanted
Not engaged but she busy doing for the D challenge
How 'bout we make a challenge for our children to be
   challenged?
Overcome the odds of black people getting married
Probably tell me suck my mother 'cause you don't know
   where your dad is
And I feel it for you, just be the man of the house
Don't let the streets abhor you
Blood of a king, heart of a slave, you should keep it royal
Don't let the streets employ you

'Cause that's a slippery slope, and it's either grease or oil
Until you hit the soil, did you reap what you sow soon as
    the reaper's got you?
I've been there, got the T-shirt, rest in peace the moral
I know it seems immoral, but degrees are optional
So we don't read, we follow
So don't tell me stay woke when I ain't slept in three days
Say I sold my soul, I want my cheque from eBay
If you love the rapper, then respect the DJ
'Cause without one, you couldn't mic-check the replay
If I was a player, man, I'd probably take the knee
I'm no longer a player, soon I'd probably take the knee
I'm shooting through the hoop, I'm trying to make a
    baby free
Already got a major team, I'm trying to make a major league
So would you rather mud on your jeans or blood on your
    leaves?
I've seen my mother cry when her little brother deceased
I'm family-orientated, I have to uncle my niece
This type of outgoings, you never underachieve
Still felt like the gift when there was nothing under the tree
My poor mother told us that nothing's coming for free
Now the show's sold out, everybody's coming for 3
And I can see your heart, and it's barely touching your sleeve
Don't tell me about circumference, that ain't circumference
    to me
I'm from the type of circle we circle up then we leave

And this squared circle ain't WWE
Keep acting like you're raw, you'll get smacked down in
the streets
All I see is fuckery every time on the news
The hurricane really just took their lives and their roof
Their whole life, all of their family under one roof
God made the wind blow and it really took 'em to you
I guess he must be missing an angel, we got a few
That shooter out in Vegas, he really gambled with youth
To even out the odds, shoulda let me snap him in two
And fight fire with electric and shock him out of his shoes
Charlie, that's me!

I'll get you hit before it hits
Don't ask me about the balloons because I was it before It
And if they don't say I'm nice then they didn't play it thrice

There's often a cycle to my rhymes. I'll open a song, and then close it, with death. I suppose it's only natural that I think about the creative process in relation to the life cycle. I definitely wasn't the first to do it: Shakespeare wrote, 'All the world's a stage', and we each have our entrance and our exit, just like actors. The curtain rises, and the curtain falls. Ashes to ashes, dust to dust. This gives you structure when you're writing a freestyle. You start thinking about how things will connect up internally. What's the beginning, middle and end, and what journey are you taking the listener on? Just because a freestyle doesn't have a bridge or a chorus, doesn't mean it shouldn't develop. Ultimately, though, it's the complexity of your lyrics in your thought patterns which builds the song up rather than gear shifts in the music itself.

Both 'Fire in the Booth pt 3' and 'Fire in the Booth pt 4' open with references to death. But there are key differences in what kind of death is being depicted. And this has implications for the direction each song takes, and the feel of them in general.

The first line of 'Fire in the Booth pt 3' goes 'Not another nigga, nah, not another nigga / Dropped on the front line with a cop behind the trigger'. It's like I'm the director of a film, and the very first scene is on a raging battlefield. It begins *in medias res*, which means 'in the middle of the action'. Because when you're born black in a racist society, you don't get the time to adjust to it. It's there from the get-go, and you'd better learn to either adapt or fight back. There's an American philosophy called *afro-pessimism* which says that to be black is characterised by being in close proximity to death. And that's how it's been throughout history. First it was with slavery, and the untold lives lost during the Middle Passage; then it was under Jim Crow segregation, and the lynchings which took place across the American South; and now it's with institutionally racist police forces who are able to kill people with impunity.

That's not just in the US either. Remember Mark Duggan. Remember Jermaine Baker. Remember Azelle Rodney. It can feel as though there's a war on the streets, except the state is fighting its own people. Black lives, especially ones which are associated with poorer areas, are treated as disposable ('Throw your spirit in the sky, probably drop you down and snigger').

After those lines, I start exploring the way in which I internalise that societal death wish: drinking. The bar 'That's why every drop of Henny's like a shot inside my liver' is like a condensed version of the sentiment I explore in 'Upon Reflection'. I'm pouring a shot, to drink a shot, for someone's that's been shot. I'm playing around with *homonyms* (same words, different meanings) to transpose the deadliness from a bullet to a beverage. It's like that headshot pun from Kendrick's 'Swimming Pools'.

Except instead of getting lost in the sauce, and letting alcohol affect the cohesion of the song, it's like I metabolise it. I reaffirm my worth as an artist ('Certain I'm the difference, but they'll probably beg to differ'), and then the Henny that I drink gets transformed into the lyrics that I spit: 'Tryna spit my thousand words before they crop me out the picture'. I want a chance to write in the history books before my image gets erased. That's the line which connects the theme of proximity to death with my work as an artist. Because my greatest fear is of dying with lyrics still left in me. How can your spirit rise up if it's weighed down by unfulfilled potential? Maybe that's a very artistic way to think about things, to treat a lack of creative expression as though you're being buried alive. Perhaps there's a fear, deep down, that to live a life in obscurity is not to live a life at all.

In 'Fire in the Booth pt 4', the depiction of death is much less violent, but a lot more uncanny: 'Lately death's been getting ever so close / Been feeling spirits while I'm driving, I should get me a ghost'. I'd been feeling that way for some years, I'd been living my life in the shadow of the valley of death. So many people I knew were dying. Unnatural, unexplained deaths. Richard Antwi went to sleep and didn't wake up. Syreta, N15's big sister, went to sleep and didn't wake up. It wasn't a disease, wasn't a car crash, it wasn't murder. It was impossible to get my head around. Usually I'm very open about death. I'm happy to talk about it. But at that point, it just felt like it was getting too close, like something could reach out and tap my shoulder at any moment. I wasn't running away from it, but I had to try and avoid it. It felt like being haunted. Or hunted.

Conveying that sentiment was really helped along by the instrumental I chose to rap on. Because even though freestyles are a showcase and exercise for your lyricism, the music is an integral part of how successful you are at telling your story. It's the table for your feast. On 'Fire in the Booth pt 4', the track is straight to the point. When I first thought about using the XX 'Intro' instrumental, I chopped it up, as if I was making a song. So it rises when the lyrics rise, and it falls when the lyrics fall. It's more of a journey. When I first listened to it, I couldn't wait to perform it, in the booth. When I was rapping along in my house, I could tell it was something different. It felt different. The way the lyrics travelled with the music had a certain kind of power. If I heard a sick rapper perform a sick rendition of one of my songs, I would respect it. But perhaps I would respect them more if they were a singer, rather than a rapper. I haven't heard anything personally from the XX. They might like it, they might not.

It's funny that even though the song opens on a dark note, there's a lot of humour in that particular freestyle. Part of it comes from having Avelino in the booth with me, and getting his reaction to the bars on the freestyle. It's like what the audience is feeling is playing out in his facial expressions, so they can see themselves in him. Also with the following lines – 'Growing up, didn't know the difference 'tween the road and my home / Now I'm grown, I'm trying to buy every home on my road' – I was just trying to be slick, really. I'm pointing out how funny it is when your perspective changes, from wanting to be as many steps away from your house as possible to wanting all the rungs on the property ladder you can manage! But thinking about the feeling of wanting to escape something that's after you, I'm also talking about the irony of wanting to be out of the house when you're young, and wanting the opposite when you're older. First it's Mum trying to get her hands on you, and then it's the Grim Reaper!

I don't open with death on 'Fire in the Booth pt 5', but I do start with a moment of stillness: 'Wrote this in the country, I was staring at horses'. Compared to the other openers, this one is a bit surreal. The visual picture I paint makes a jokey little contrast between where I'm recording 'Fire in the Booth pt 5' – in the middle of a city, in a studio that's considered the cradle of urban music – and what I'm rapping about. It's a dissonant image. But's actually true – I started working on the lyric when we were on residential making the FR32 album. There was a stable between the studio and the house, and because the studio had see-through walls, you'd just be rapping while having a staring contest with a horse. Sometimes you'd play a beat, and I swear they'd be dancing!

It was a million miles away from glamour and clubs, but it was what I needed to make music at that time: 'It's kinda nice to be still, I've been Frankie detouring'. The second part of that line is supposed to be a little nod to the honourable Frankie Dettori, the jockey. It links back to the bit about horses, but it's also a foreshadowing of what comes next. Frankie Dettori is, or at least he used to be, a notorious playboy. He was all about Ferraris and glamour and getting into trouble.

So turning his name into a verb ('frankly detouring')

tells you something about the way I'd been living: 'I left my soul in every city, it's sad but it's honest / The amount of morning-after pills, I should have an endorsement'. That's a pretty revealing bar in any song, let alone a Fire in the Booth. The moment of stillness in the country has allowed me the space to reflect on all the running up and down that I was doing. Working. Touring. Sleeping around. When I was in the middle of my rampage era, that line would've been a boast. Now I'm looking back, I can see the tragedy in it.

Normally, sex is seen as something from which men gain and women lose. Here, I'm flipping the stereotype. It's me who's left feeling hollow. Reggie Yates was the one to say it to me: 'Don't you think you lose a part of yourself every time?' Back then, I was like, 'Nah! What more could I want?' But when you get a bit of distance from living like that, you realise there's something wrong about being able to walk past someone and remember an encounter, but not a name.

There's a doubleness in those bars as well. When I talk about 'detouring' and 'I left my soul in every city', I'm also talking about literally touring. When you're in front of a crowd, it's like you're giving everything of yourself over to them. It's passionate. It's intimate. And then the next night, you move on to another town and you do it all over again. How much is too much? You feel exposed, especially when that boundary between artist and audience is getting crossed before and after the show. It's exhausting, so there's a parallel with promiscuity that I'm trying to draw there.

All three of these openings touch on different themes and different moods, but all in their own way are trying to achieve the same thing. Fire in the Booth is competitive. They sometimes record a few of them on the same day, so maybe you see another artist coming out just as you're going in. You start wondering, 'How good was their one?' And Charlie Sloth doesn't help with the old flame on gas mark 6: he loves introducing different beats, showing his appreciation through ad-libs and exclamations, wheeling up the track. But you have to focus on what you came there to do, at all times, and not let a reload or a sound effect throw you off. The discipline is to carve out a bit of space for stillness. You can do that with your choice of beat, you can do it with your verse, or you can just do it with your demeanour. When you've combined all three, they'll defo remember not to forget you. It's the ability to create serenity within chaos that separates the good from the great when they step into the booth.

When you're doing a Fire in the Booth you have to demonstrate versatility without introducing gimmicks for the sake of it. Each MC has their own approach when trying to achieve this. So maybe they'll use multiple tracks, or record for a longer time or do a few takes. That's never been me, though. I don't like faffing about with three different beats. Because we're finishing this inside ninety minutes, we're not going to penalties. I don't want extra time.

The way I try and introduce variety in my freestyle is strictly verbal. It's all about structure, wordplay and thematic content. One way to keep things moving is to switch up my accent mid-verse. I do it in 'Fire in the Booth pt 4' when I say: 'The less mercy you show could leave you merciless alone / But I'm yard grown, so I ain't taking no badda, nah'. It's just for the second bar, but it changes the vibe completely. Because of my Jamaican background, I find it's very natural for me to switch accents. It's not like I'm doing something artificial, it's just what I know.

My mum will speak in an English accent when she's speaking to us or to her friends from work. But if she calls my auntie, she switches to patois. It's code switching, a way of communicating with your people, a way of feeling connected to your heritage when it extends beyond the shores of Britain. But it's not a conscious thing when I do it. It just pops out when I'm recording. It sort of doubles the language available. Patois has its own rhythms and rhyme schemes, its own flexibility. So you might not be able to rhyme something in straight English – and then patois opens a door for you.

I reckon you can tell a lot about what kind of music an MC grew up with based on how they use patois in their songs. Because patois isn't just something we heard from our parents, it's on the records they kept in the house – reggae, dancehall, ragga, that kind of thing. The way I use patois is very similar to Beenie Man, because he was the main guy in my house when I was young. But when I hear Flowdan, for instance, I hear a lot of Bounty Killer, so I wonder if that's what he grew up listening to. Hopefully one day I'll get to ask him! Either way, patois is something I use most when I'm describing home, because that's where it comes from. It's a way of gesturing to how I was raised. Just a little thing, but it's effective.

Diversity in delivery is one way you can introduce an element of the unexpected into a freestyle. Another is wordplay. Best of all is when you can find an original way to say that you're the most original rapper out there. It's like a king declaring war: you're doing the thing in the very act of saying the thing. So in 'Fire in the Booth pt 4', I make the point by starting from a position of insecurity: 'I mean, how many more gems can I drop on the future? / How much of my fans just might not buy my new stuff?' On one hand, there's the pressure to perform and generate new material; and on the other, there's the risk that what I do is so new it alienates the audience I already have. It's a dilemma that almost every artist has to grapple with in their career.

I'll always come down on the side of taking risks. I hope people who liked my early stuff could still hear 'Don't Go' or '6 Words' and realise I'm a proper musician. You've got to have ambition. I'm lucky in that I've always been encouraged in what I want to do. Imagine what might have happened if Stormzy's bredrins had said, 'Bro, why are you making "Blinded by Your Grace"?' I think black artists are imprisoned by genre. No one thinks of The Beatles as just a guitar band. As a black artist, everything you do has to be twice as good. You can't shy away from it. The cream of the crop will remain. You have to always care, and want to push beyond what people see you as. Imagine what would have been lost if certain artists were discouraged from pursuing their ambitions. I've been lucky. Twin B, who's my A&R and also co-head of A&R at Atlantic, has always told me, 'You've got to try it. What have you come to do? Are you here to do half of what you're capable of? Or are you here to surpass what you're capable of?' It's ambition. The only person who can stop you from fulfilling your ambition, really, is you.

In 'Fire in the Booth pt 4', I try and subtly make this point through my wordplay. I move from that statement of self-doubt to a celebration of self-sufficiency and risk-taking: 'We all got bars, but nobody here's a brewer / Bringing sandwich to the beach in the hope of finding tuna'. When I say 'We all got bars', I'm talking about the way in which you become a machine when you attain a certain level of success. A lot of musicians I see at that level seem to be striving only to set records. They have the winning formula, they just have to keep pumping out new music. It's like a microwave – you put the food in, set the timer, and the job's done. You've got an endless supply of bars, but they're all the same bar. That's not the same as being 'a brewer', as in being able to sustain yourself from your own well of creativity.

The following bar is playing on a well-known idiom. Instead of 'bringing sand to the beach' – which means contributing nothing of value because that thing already exists – you bring a 'sandwich to the beach in the hope of finding tuna'. It means that I'm bringing something different in order to win a bigger prize. There's also a bit of a warning in there too: not every risk you take will pay off. You have to reject the safety and familiarity of what's already been done for its own sake. It won't always work out, especially if you haven't put the work in properly. But also, these bars are just a bit of fun. It's something I enjoy doing – taking words and phrases that you already know, and rejigging them to suit my own purposes.

I do know, though, that there is a push and pull between creativity and the commercial side of music. And it's in that tension that you have to shape a career for yourself. Later on in 'Fire in the Booth pt 4', I'm acknowledging the fact that critics have often found it difficult to get their heads around the range of styles in my work. Because there's a general consensus amongst the critics that my lyricism and flow put me on a par with the greatest rappers in the world ('And this will be the best Fire in the Booth / And I doubt they'll tell you different when I'm standing in the room'). But because some of my records don't always have the same venom or display the same amount of skill, it's considered less boundary-pushing.

I've already talked about how I don't like being limited in terms of genre, and that's something I'm referring to in the bars 'Why? Different class / Sometimes you have to ask: / "Do you want to be the best in your country or your school?"' A big fish in a small pond can't see much of the horizon. Whereas I know there's a whole ocean out there. This sentiment comes from never accepting anything less than the best. I do think we have a habit of rewarding mediocrity, or celebrating effort, as opposed to celebrating success. Don't get me wrong, England had a wonderful run in the World Cup, but we really should have been in the final. We could have won. Let's celebrate what we achieved, but let's not settle for less. We've got a phenomenal squad, and deserve to be there. But there's also a more pragmatic reason for me making records intended to sell well: 'In a country full of rules, where we're selling lollipop to keep them sucking on our balls'. There're commercial concerns in music, undoubtedly. It's the sugar rush we're pushing, sometimes. It's necessary, but it's a compromise. It's what you have to do to keep the scene alive.

If you want to sustain the freedom to be avant-garde, you've got to have a certain level of financial security. The ideal scenario for a musician is getting to a point where you don't have to take money into account. But not everyone can enjoy that luxury. Maybe the best rapper in the world is someone you've never heard of. Maybe they're on a street corner somewhere, struggling to pay for studio time. Jay-Z is someone who understands this acutely. He rapped about it on 'Moment of Clarity':

> I dumbed down for my audience to double my dollars
> They criticized me for it, yet they all yell 'holla'
> If skills sold, truth be told, I'd probably be lyrically
>   Talib Kweli
> Truthfully I wanna rhyme like Common Sense
> But I did 5 mill' – I ain't been rhyming like Common
>   since

He's admitting that finance has affected his artistic style, but it's a conscious choice he made so that he wasn't just relegated to the lower leagues.

This is not to say you become undiscerning. You have to be careful with what you're seen to endorse. You have to think about these things carefully. I never really looked into horse racing, for example, but I went to Ascot one day, and posted a picture, and had a lot of people in my comments saying, 'Wait, how can you support people whipping horses?' I hadn't really thought about it. I don't agree with it. I'm a pescatarian. I'll never take that risk with a record. Never with a song. As part of a campaign? Maybe. But the record's the only reason they want you in their advert in the first place. So if you start reworking the songs, then what happens? After 'Traktor', we got a lot of approaches. Swedish House Mafia got in touch, for example, and sent over some songs. I met them, and liked them, but I just didn't get the music. I didn't do it, and I don't regret it. It wasn't meant to be.

I guess the key is to keep your integrity, but never let anyone else decide what your integrity is. My desire to be the best rapper is matched by my desire to be the best songwriter, regardless of genre. If I was afraid of displaying this, I'd kill my success before it could even draw breath. If that makes you uncomfortable, then all I can say is that I'm sorry your short-sightedness prevents you from seeing the scale of my vision.

Even when it's nonsense, wordplay is never pointless. It's like I was saying before with the turn of the Rubik's cube: you're not just looking to show off your technical brilliance, you're showing that you can find instability in language in a strategic way. One way or another, your creativity has to be the thing which acts as connective tissue, linking up a story, a theme or a thought pattern. So continuing the theme of ambition in 'Fire in the Booth pt 4', I talk about having the kind of mentality where I know my worth in spite of what others are telling me: 'Fuck that, even when I lose, I'm the winner'. I've always been competitive. But I've never felt like I've lost, even if someone has surpassed me. The first time I was made to feel like a loser was when I went to the MOBOs. We'd done so much, and we were as big as we could possibly get. Nominated for four awards, and I didn't win one. You feel inadequate. I might not be in competition with Ghetts, but if he wins that award, I lose. We need to take something back from the awards. We can't look to awards for validation.

Instead of buying into petty competitiveness, I celebrate just how far my people have come: 'tried to minus my pluses just to divide my people / Who go from stepping on roaches to stepping by The Beatles'. If you view your community as crabs in a barrel, all you can do is tear down the people who look like you and let those in power off the hook for putting you in that position in the first place. I'm using the roaches/Beatles pun to say that the ability to go from the margins of society to the centre of popular culture is an absolute triumph. I don't believe that applauding other people's achievements is a display of weakness. Because my accomplishments speak for themselves, I can use my platform to write our whole scene into the history books ('They say my weakness is kindness / I kill them with success, 'cause it's timeless'). In my eyes, that's 'progression at its finest'.

That's when the wordplay comes in. I put together a pantheon of the greats so that I can place myself in their company. If sticking to one genre means you're just a big fish in a small pond, here I'm swimming with sharks. The word 'progression' signals the technique that follows, where I use allusion and *homophones* (words that sound similar) to turn classic braggadocio into a more interesting statement of where I see myself as an artist:

> *The writing's on the wall, we know who Destiny's Child is*
> *King Kendrick or Jermaine Cole*
> *Or are you saying 'King Wretched' or 'Jermaine's Cold'?*
> *I'm trying to lay the blueprint and give you reasonable doubt*
> *So when you watch the throne, they can see me change clothes*

The names and albums I reference here provide a model to aspire towards, and also a reminder of what's required. I mean, how much bigger can you get? Jay-Z is for ever. He's someone who's shown how you can adapt over your career, without losing what makes you *you*. In fact, every time he changed something about his craft, whether it was style or content, he somehow became more himself. That's not just in the later years, like revealing his vulnerability on 4:44. Early on in his career, he made the decision to deliberately slow down his tempo. It wasn't because he was bad at rapping fast – if you search on YouTube you can find videos from the 1990s where his pace is just insane – but because he wanted people to hear more of what he had to say. That's the kind of longevity and thoughtfulness I consider myself capable of. And if I wanted to, I could convey this sentiment in a straightforward way. I could just say, 'Kendrick, Jay-Z, J Cole: they're my guys.' But if I actually want to put myself on their level, I need to show skill and ambition in how I put that point across. That's why I let the bars build up: I'm providing the proof of what I'm saying.

The way I link images, allusions and idioms together is my signature move. Because lots of writers pile similes on top of similes, metaphors on top of metaphors, but I've not seen anyone pay attention to the transition in the way I do. I've looked it up in poetry books and anthologies of literature studies: there's just no word for what I do. Because most figurative language is concerned with fixing an image in your mind's eye. It's like trying to take a photograph with words. What I'm trying to do is paint a picture of movement. It's like alchemy – I'm fascinated by how you can turn one thing into another, as though you've managed to catch language in the very act of its own evolution. I call it *transmutation*: in physics, it refers to one element transforming into another, but the alchemists of the medieval period used it to refer to their impossible dream of turning lead into gold.

It's a technique you see at its full stretch in 'Fire in the Booth pt 5'. First, I start talking about the combination of isolation and socialising that you experience as an artist: 'They don't tell you how to live your dream without the sleep / How on the weekend you're the man but it gets lonely in the week'. This is something I've talked with Avelino about – everyone will be blowing up his phone on Friday and Saturday, 'cause they want the action and the raving, but it'll all go quiet come Monday. There's nothing you can do about it, other than make yourself emotionally resilient enough to cope with the contrast. If you want a different kind of lifestyle, go work in human resources! After I've explored the realm of friendship, I move on to talking about family:

> No surrender, no retreat, some family on your tree now
> Can only see your branch when they used to hear your leaves
> Used to share your feast
> Then no one was hungry soon as the GOAT became the sheep

In 'Fire in the Booth pt 5' I use a sample from Billie Holiday's 'Strange Fruit'; it's at this point in the freestyle where the lyrics of my rap and the words from the sample start to overlap. It's a subtle way of nurturing variety and encouraging thoughtful listening when you do a Fire in the Booth. Like sometimes the beat is just a backing track, and sometimes it's in conversation with your lyrics. You have to pay attention! I'm taking the image of the family tree, and then saying they 'can only see your branch when they used to hear your leaves'. So, people used to value what I could create naturally rather than what was in my bank branch. That pun is undergirded by the poetic contrast between lush and supple leaves, and the rigid and hard branch. Texture is important here. The movement between the two helps create the mood, while the plaintive tone of Billie Holiday's voice heightens the sense of sadness.

Then the rhyme of 'leaves' with 'feast' allows me to

pursue a different set of puns and metaphors. No one wants to know the Greatest Of All Time ('the GOAT') when he loses his status and becomes just another figure in the herd ('the sheep'). It's another moment of transmutation. The GOAT turning into a sheep is like Cinderella's carriage turning into a pumpkin after midnight. It's a spell wearing off, a returning to form. There's a little hint of The Last Supper here when I talk about feasting: the sense of a generous figure at the centre of the table who's about to be betrayed. You're never more paranoid than when you're at your peak. Ninety-nine per cent of the people you met on your way up won't be around on your way down. It's like Fortune's Wheel – it's when you're at the top that you're destined for a fall, and no one wants to be around to help you break it.

I'm saying that I'm not even going to get involved in that game. If everyone's at the feast, tearing into GOATs and sheep, 'I'm pescatarian', I'm opting out entirely. The fish imagery here is my Get Out of Jail Free card. I can't be on the menu, because I'm already swimming away in a different current:

> That's why I'm pescatarian, it was sink or swim in
>   the aquarium
> Either break the glass or you share with them
> Shots at me but I can only give what I receive
> There's gunpowder on my clothes now, washing my machine

The rhyme scheme at the end of the line here becomes a more traditional couplet structure, which gives me the scaffolding I require in order to escape the need to be strictly literal in my language. The cadence changes so that what I say has more of a punch to it.

This whole section is a constant acceleration of intensity. So the pescatarian at the table becomes the fish in the aquarium. Rather than let that image sit in stillness and embellish it with more detail, I set about transforming it yet again. It's dog-eat-dog (or fish-eat-fish) in this little box, because you force yourself into fighting for scarce resources when you stay in a smaller space. The glass walls of the fish tank are a prison, so I've got to smash them to pieces in order to make it to the mainstream.

But once more, I don't follow the image to a logical conclusion (fish flopping on the floor, or making a *Finding Nemo* escape into the ocean). I use the kinetic energy of the shattered aquarium to take me to a different plane of escalation. I imagine it was bullets that smashed the aquarium ('Shots at me but I can only give what I receive'), and I'm firing those same rounds back at the shooter. It's like I've had a curse lifted, and turned back from a fish into a man. The aquarium becomes a swirling washing machine. I've defeated my enemy and now I'm cleaning the evidence off my gun ('There's gunpowder on my clothes now, washing my machine').

Feel breathless? Good, can I get an ahhh yeaaaa! I've learned not to worry too much about going over the heads of my audience. That's the point of transmutation: it's about not being afraid of the poetic potential that exists within language. You locate it, you activate it, and you set off a chain reaction in your bars. Transmutation isn't like a traditional literary technique, because it's not just one thing. It's a combination of all the tools a writer has available to them in order for their verse to be dynamic, explosive and unexpected. Whoever's gonna get it, is gonna get it. And who doesn't get it should be *feeling* it regardless.

Transmutation as a technique demonstrates dexterity and flair, but this doesn't mean you can't use it to make serious points as well. In 'Open Conversation & Mark Duggan', I talk about turning the hangman's rope into 'straight white gold', to show how I'm trying to create something positive out of a devastating tragedy. Or in 'Fire in the Booth pt 3', I use it to make a moral point:

> *I grew up in a maze, where I saw cats chasing their tails*
> *Dogs selling to cats, man killing their dogs*
> *The lost think that they're found, the found think that*
>   *they're God*
> *Fighting over ground, but to none of us it belongs*

And the cons outweigh the pros, but the pros can weigh
   an oz
And turn coke into powder, that's just connecting the dots
Man, now are you tempted to shot?

The twists and turns of the maze are mirrored in the
way I follow my train of thought. There's a persistent
sense of futility – there's no journey up, only violence
that doubles back on itself. The maze you're trapped in,
and trapping in, doesn't even belong to you. What's the
point in fighting over territory when gentrification is
just going to push you out of the neighbourhood
anyway? The cocaine powder you're selling has the
potential to turn into gunpowder at any second:
shotting is only ever a heartbeat away from being shot.
I'm not trying to preach here – I'm 'just connecting the
dots'. The technique of transmutation allows me to
expose what's already there in my set-up, rather than
having to interject with something new.

There are times, however, when you have to break
up the structure in a freestyle. Wordplay allows you to
explore multiple themes within a single set-up, but
sometimes you need to create the space to explore one
thing with the depth and the gravity it deserves. Some
things don't sit well as an aside. When I talk about the
passing of Richard Antwi in 'Fire in the Booth pt 3',
I dedicate a whole section to giving him an appropriate

elegy. Because he wasn't just a music lawyer; he was a star behind the scenes. He was our guiding light, our philosopher. That's why I quote him in the freestlye: 'Rich said, "Who wakes up and really wants to come second?"' I want his words to live for ever.

Richard was a treasure whose value defied pricing – you could only measure him the same way you'd count your blessings. 'Ever lost someone who found you with intentions on bringing something out of you to turn you to a legend?' – I'm trying to communicate the sense of utter devastation I felt at losing the person who'd helped me find my own direction in life. And I know I'm not the only one. So many artists who made their way into the 1Xtra studio got their launch from Richard. He carried the whole scene on his shoulders: you'd find it hard to name a UK rapper who doesn't have a good story about him.

But because it's Fire in the Booth, it was important to deliver this elegy in a personal way. So I invite the listener to share in the moment of my grief: 'When I heard the news I had to park up on the kerb / I was on the phone to Twin, and we didn't even say a word'. Because when something actually hits me hard, I won't cry. I'll sit in silence and feel the darkness closing in. That's how it was when I heard the news about Richard. I was in my car and Twin had called me up, and we both just sat on the line and listened to nothing. Even after

I hung up and drove off, it felt like I was carrying that silence with me. But it was in solitude I realised that what I had to do was celebrate the impact Richard Antwi had had on all of us: 'Spend time alone, see I just had to define life / The good die young, so your calling was primetime'.

And the best way to celebrate Richard's life is to carry on his legacy of mentoring young artists. It's the right thing to do. You have to share what you know. It's like, imagine if Pelé had been watching Messi doing kick-ups as a kid. Pelé could walk by, and Messi would achieve greatness, eventually, or Pelé could stop and give Messi a few tips, put him in contact with a few people, buy him some boots, and maybe he achieves greatness a little sooner. And that's why I've taken such an interest in taking Avelino under my wing. He's a graduate from the school of Wretch. The mentoring process is a lesson in both directions. I teach, he learns, but I also get schooled by the student. He's a good example of what can happen when you work hard, and you think hard. When we first started speaking, what surprised me was how much he had studied. He didn't just know a few of my lyrics, he knew every word. He'd done his homework. It's been incredible to see him succeed. He's mad talented. We both have a similar mindset and a way of speaking now. Like, we definitely both use too many analogies. He's like a sparring partner. When I want to fight, I fight him. It's the only way to improve. I want him to shine. I told him before our Fire in the Booth, 'Listen to me very carefully. Make sure your verse is as good as it can be. We only get one chance.'

At the same time, I recognise that at some point, he has to take over. One day he'll chop my head off. And I always say, when that day comes, embrace it. You can't become the king without your father dying. It's just not gonna be today, Av!

I used to get labelled in that bracket of being a 'conscious rapper'. I never really liked it, because who's to say that something is 'unconscious'? Maybe it's not the case that an artist is ignoring politics or what else is going on in the world. Maybe they're just putting it across in a way you don't understand. But I do think the role of artists is to be closer to history than they are to the media cycle. I prefer to speak about things in a song. I have time to think about what I think about. I have time to think about what I want to say, and how I want to say it. What's the best mode of communication for this particular issue? If I feel strongly about something, music is the best medium for me. It's not a question, it's not a quiz. You can take what you want from it, but I know at least I've said what I wanted to say.

Sometimes, like in 'Fire in the Booth pt 3', I'll tee it

up ('And if it gets political, call me Tony Blair Witch'),
but just leave my political comment there as a question
('Why did we vote Leave? Why did we vote Leave?').
Because I'm not really there to get into the nitty-gritty
of Westminster shenanigans. I'm more interested
in how ordinary people are being sold out by the
system:

> The government's sending kids to sleep with no dreams
> They're trying to tick a box, you would have thought they
>   sold weed
> Everybody's high, no wonder why the future's codeine

So what I'm saying here is that the government has
given up on actually trying to make things better for
people. Instead, all we've got are things intended to
pacify us. The little pun on future/codeine is a nod to
the rapper, but also a reference to the idea that our best
hope for the future might be anaesthesia. Fall asleep
and numb the pain.

I think more people are aware of politics now.
Whether it's because of social media or whether there's
some broader shift, I think people are more conscious
of what's going on, and how it affects them. But I don't
think politics is getting better. Some things are so mad.
With modern slavery, for example. It's one thing to even
comprehend what's happening, let alone think about

what has to be done to stop it. How is this even a thing? It's very dark. There are so many things that I want to jump into, but I don't know what it will do to me. It sounds like a selfish thing to say, but I feel that in trying to do something positive, or proactive, I might create harm somehow. Whether it's to myself, or to someone else.

Sometimes it's hard to even want to contribute something constructive to a debate. At the end of 'Fire in the Booth pt 5' I talk about how I feel when 'All I see is fuckery every time on the news'. Because when you turn on the TV, it's never the rich and powerful who are suffering, it's the poor. It feels like every summer, more and more hurricanes are ravaging the Caribbean. And you see these places, which are meant to be like paradise, reduced to ruin within a couple of days: 'The hurricane really just took their lives and their roof / Their whole life, all of their family under one roof'. Here I'm talking about Hurricane Maria, but it could be about any of them since Katrina. It's a similar thing with the line 'That shooter out in Vegas, he really gambled with youth'. It refers to a shooting that happened a couple of weeks before I recorded the Fire in the Booth, but it's something that happens all too frequently in America. With gun laws being what they are, they're as reckless with people's lives as a gambling addict is with their chips.

It's telling that we've stopped being able to remember the names of every gunman who's committed a mass shooting. We just say where it happened. It shouldn't be the kind of thing you get desensitised to. So when I bring it up, I'm literally trying to bring back the shock factor: 'To even out the odds, shoulda let me snap him in two / And fight fire with electric and shock him out of his shoes'. I'm not holding back on the frustration and the rage I feel when I see a news story like that. I'm articulating the very human feeling of wanting retribution. To even up the odds against the man who fired round after round into a defenceless crowd, I don't want to fight fire with fire. I want to fight fire with electricity! It's just me expressing what I feel rather than trying to offer a concrete solution.

That's the thing about my approach to Fire in the Booth. I'm not trying to explain how the world works to you. I'm trying to show you what my perspective is, where I am in life, and what my thought patterns are. Others might want to hold a mirror up to society; my priority is to reflect my state of mind. So any social commentary I offer is pulled through the prism of my own experience. When it comes to the ending of 'Fire in the Booth pt 4', this means I'm tying together two things I feel very strongly about: how the police treat people, and how artists are being gradually squeezed out of being able to live off their work.

I found it quite startling how everyone rushed to drag Tidal when it got launched, and so I really wanted to comment on that: 'And Tidal's got the whole world moving crazy / It's like they rather a free Spotify playlist'. I think part of it is just the whole social media thing of trying to pull someone down when they're stepping out of the box you want to put them in. So people looked at Jay-Z trying to do something new, and were like, 'Who does this black man think he is, Steve Jobs?' But that's an injustice in my book. That's why I link it to 'them cops on the day shift / Who just can't stop and search without tasing'. Because social negativity and institutional racism are both designed to do the same thing: keep people down.

The electric shock from a taser transmutes into the emotion of shock:

> *Shit seems shocking when you're reading about it*
> *Six years old they was raiding my house, shit*
> *Tryna find my uncle, didn't open my mouth, shit*

I'm going back to a childhood memory, when we had one of my uncles from Jamaica staying with us. I don't know what he did, and never asked, but we were raided. I was young, but I knew we didn't speak to the police. Ever. I remember thinking, 'Well, why can't we just say that he was here?' But I didn't question it. It wasn't just a

way of thinking, it was a way of life. It's not me and my
friends versus the cops. Our family's survival depends
on me not speaking to the cops.

From there, we move back to the music industry. You
know me and my word association:

> The Titanic ain't going down because of me
> See, I can't swim, but I'll be the anchor for the scene
> See, how do they expect musicians to stay afloat
> When all our sales keep going down the stream?

The police theme is a bit of a diversion, but the idea
of 'loose lips sink ships' comes back to the water
imagery of Tidal, which comes back to what I was
trying to articulate at the beginning of the whole thing.
Everything's connected. Nothing is thrown away in a
Fire in the Booth. It all comes back. It's an important
point. How the fuck do they expect us to survive? People
are spending £9.99 per month, and artists are getting
0.0001p per play. You have to have a million plays to
see any money. There is one streaming service that is
artist-owned, that's paying the highest royalties to
artists, but everyone is against it. I don't get it. Those
lines speak to my frustrations about that particular
situation. Someone is trying to do right by artists,
and being attacked for it. You might prefer one platform
over another: fine. But why attack the platform that's

supporting artists? You don't know the ins and outs of it! Labels own shares in certain platforms! They are eating twice!

Every Fire in the Booth I've done closes a loop by taking you the whole way round a track. So perhaps I open with death, and I close with the struggle for survival. Or perhaps I open with stillness in the countryside, and I leave you with the shooting in Las Vegas. I'm showing you how these things are connected, but I'm also giving you variety. Just because you begin and end in darkness doesn't mean there can't be light along the way. I'm at my best in a Fire in the Booth because I've got the freedom to explore my worst. You have to dig deep to find gems. These freestyles are studies in contrast; and similarly, the progression from Chapter 1 to here took you from 'Pisces' in the sea to spitting Fire in the Booth. It's the journey from the classroom to the court of the king.

But while we've reached the pinnacle, don't think we've reached the end. The confessional booth is just a rehearsal for a coffin. You're drafting what you'll say when it comes to your last breath.

OUTRO: THE COFFIN

Do you ever feel like you've already seen the end? With me, I want to create from every aspect and every angle, so I try and think everything through. That's the way it is with every project I've ever worked on: I want full control from conception to completion. And I feel the same way about death. I've even planned out my own funeral. I mean, I want to design it! That might sound morbid to modern ears, because as a society we don't deal with death very well. But it wasn't always like that.

In Ancient Egypt, death was a part of everyday life. It was a normal thing to prepare for your burial while you were still healthy, and people would chat, like, 'How's your tomb coming along?' Death wasn't seen as a permanent ending: it was more like walking through a door into another form of existence. That's why tombs were full of household objects as well as treasures: the idea was that the departed would need all that stuff in the afterlife. People still grieved for the loss of their loved ones, that's just human nature, but death wasn't seen as a taboo thing to talk about. It was meticulously prepared for.

I share a lot of that attitude to death. Not like I'm

building a tomb or planning to get mummified, but I definitely think about it every day. I've always got one eye on my legacy – when I die, my music will be all that's left of me. But it also guides how I make music. You never know when you're going to go. I said earlier in this book that my greatest fear is dying with lyrics still left inside me, that I'm scared I won't be able to rest if something's gone unsaid. That's a sentiment that's shared in a lot of different cultures. For Catholics, confession in life is important so you don't die with sins left on your soul. But a really interesting one, again, is how the Ancient Egyptians thought about it.

In *The Egyptian Book of the Dead*, it's written that after death, a person's soul would be taken to meet Osiris, the god of the afterlife, and Thoth, the scribe of the gods. After confessing that your soul is pure, the Egyptians believed that your heart would be taken and placed on scales to be weighed against the feather of truth. If your heart was lighter than the feather, your soul could move on to live in eternal paradise. If not, it would face oblivion. I don't believe in the actual myth myself, but there's a lot that I find inspiring about it. It's a way of thinking that there's something spiritual about the act of writing or making music itself. That it's related to honesty, a quality valued above all others. When the art says yes, you can't say no because your very soul is at stake. It's not about fame or fortune, it's about integrity. I don't speak the truth in my work because I'm trying to be a prophet – I'm just trying to get it off my chest.

The only thing that's permanent in this life is impermanence. Birth is followed by death, which is followed by new life again. That nothing stays the same is probably the only certainty that you can hold on to. It's the same in music. When you write a song, you're not setting something down in stone. Every beat, every verse or bar or punchline is a living thing. As soon as you record and release it, your art stop being just yours. It belongs to the culture now, as part of a community of artists. That's why you've got to be excited about other people's work. They're not just your competition – they're your family. Your fellow creators are the only ones who understand what it's like to be serving the higher purpose of art. It's important to celebrate them.

This is one of the reasons why I think it's important to pay attention to lyrics, and what they offer. There is always something new to learn, and someone new to learn from. This is something that I will never forget.

You already know that I idolise Jay-Z, but I want to talk about artists a little closer to home. Unsurprisingly, Ghetts is one of my peers whose work I really admire. He's got all the ingredients of a great rapper: passion, aggression, energy and lyrics. He's one of the most technically gifted artists I can think of. It's almost impossible to single out my all-time favourite Ghetts moment, because in over ten years he just keeps producing them. Would I say it's one of the legendary battles, or a live show? A Daily Duppy, or his infamous Risky Roadz freestyle? An exciting artist is someone who gets you into arguments about what was his best work. I suppose what I respect the most is Ghetts' ability to constantly improve his work, to evolve and stay relevant. It's one thing being blessed with talent, but it's another to keep up with all of music's changes without losing what makes you who you are. That says something about the seriousness of your craft.

Ghetts understands the fundamentals of rap: no gimmicks, just impress them with words. I think part of the key that turns in the lyricist's door isn't how many stories you can tell, it's how many different ways you can tell the same one. That's how you make sixteen years feel like sixteen bars! If you go back and listen to his earlier songs, they're timeless. There's a tune called 'Convo with a Cabbie' which was way ahead of its time, one of my favourite story records ever. The way Ghetts sculpts a three-dimensional character before your very ears is just incredible, realistic and uncompromising all at once. I sometimes find myself wishing that record had been made today, and a video was shot for it. It'd be such a big deal!

Avelino is another one: a complete master when it comes to wordplay. Some artists are good rhymers and leave it at that, but Av – in my opinion – is pushing the boundaries of English literature. There's something Shakespearean about his bars. He's ambitious in his craft, and you could probably hand in his verses as A-level coursework! Avelino has that rare quality of possessing talent and intellect, but not having it go over anyone's head. His combination of old and new techniques is so exciting to hear – he treats language as elastic, and tests the limits of what it can do. In 'M.O.E (Remix)', he spits in a way that I think is really forward thinking:

> Never had a hundred pounds I'm like give me the bill
> I told her if your lad's broke, man's William Hill
> I've been in the field
> But didn't like it so I left, I started rhymin' fuck these
>   niggas, they're just pythons
> Everybody sounds-s-s-s like this-s-s-s, even when
>   they're silent
> I'm just tryna make that boss money call that M Bison

It was one of those moments when, as an artist, I was really blown away because I heard something I'd never thought of. His wordplay throughout the verse demonstrates such depth and character. The betting-shop pun of 'lad's broke' (as in Ladbrokes) into William Hill sets up the rhyme with 'field', which in turn develops the narrative. That pronunciation of the 's' is just stunning: the way he repeats it means that a sibilant 's' sound suddenly feels like a beat. It is one of my favourite moments from Avelino of all time.

Dave is an anomaly. And I mean that in the best way: in a generation where saying something with meaning and meaning what you say has almost gone out the window, along comes Santan Dave! It's thrilling to see a new writer with the essence of all the greats. I love listening to a good story delivered in a rap verse, and Dave took that one step further by delivering a solid narrative with his album *Psychodrama*. Anyone who can keep an audience on the edge of their seats, with one record that's eleven minutes long, is extremely gifted. I love who Dave is, and what he represents. He's one of the few that can push the genre beyond our expectations. It's mad that someone so young is able to combine saying something nuanced with just telling it like it is.

For instance on 'Hangman', Dave manages to deliver a really thoughtful social critique with unflinching directness. He rails against the twisted values that have young people abandoning their dreams of success for a lifestyle which will ultimately destroy them, and says: 'London is cursed, this city's got a problem / My bro ain't got a bird he got an ostrich, a fucking life sentence'. He won't let you forget that he's talking from a place of experience, not distance. The pun on 'bird', meaning time in prison as well as slang for a woman, sets up the punchline on 'ostrich'. His older brother's not got a short sentence, he's in for life: a long bird, or long stretch – an ostrich.

Stormzy, undoubtedly, is the king of the new generation. He's brave, he's fierce, and he speaks for the voiceless both on and off the mic. When you're a rapper with a huge amount of ambition, it can sometimes work against you. Being forward thinking is often misunderstood as selling out, and that's why I say that Stormzy's brave. He's been able to look past what's been expected of him, and commit to doing what *he* wants to do. People didn't want 'Blinded by Your Grace' until Stormzy gave it to them. The art said yes, and he refused to say no despite not knowing how the record would be received. That shows he's got character, determination and integrity. His vocal presence commands attention, which is half the fight won. And his lyrical content holds on to the reader's focus:

> I got smoke, you can hold a bit
> A coloured brother with a bone to pick
> But I still get to gunning, don't be running when
>   I bang mine
> Before we said our prayers, there was gang signs

Stormzy declares his statement of intent in a way that means he's impossible to ignore. That's the mark of a true leader. Speak your mind at all times; wear your art on your sleeve, and you shall never be forgotten as long as we breathe.

Art is the practice of storing experience, and using your craft to turn it into something that exists outside of yourself. Writing techniques are like genes – I've inherited some from those who came before me, but I also generated new ones which are passed down through new artists. Because that's the thing: individuals are born and die, but as long as the collective keeps evolving, we'll never go extinct. Words aren't the stuff of dusty papers on forgotten bookshelves. They move through us as breath. We only know the plays of William Shakespeare because the actors who had worked with him got together after he passed away, and recited each line from memory. It's funny how language dies as soon as it leaves your lips, but it was the spoken word that kept Shakespeare's work alive. Your life is only as important as the impact you have on the living. That's the philosophy of *Rapthology*: death only means oblivion if you don't leave anything behind that can grow after you're gone.

For a glossary, and more information on *Rapthology*,
please visit the book's page on:

www.penguin.co.uk

DISCOGRAPHY

Mixtapes

Learn from My Mixtape
Released: 2006

Teachers' Training Day
Released: 2007

Verses 3 and 2 Chapter Wretch
Released 2007

Wretch32.com
Released 2010

More Fun! (with Chipmunk)
Released: 2010

Wretchercise
Released: 2012

Young Fire, Old Flame
Released: 2015

Albums

Wretchrospective

Released: 13 October 2008
Label: Hip Hop Village/Renowned Records

Black and White
Released: 22 August 2011
Label: Ministry of Sound

Growing Over Life
Released: 2 September 2016
Label: Polydor

FR32
Released: 13 October 2017
Label: Polydor

Singles

As lead artist:

'Traktor' (featuring L)
Year: 2011
Album: *Black and White*
Certification: BPI: Gold

'Unorthodox' (featuring Example)
Year: 2011
Album: *Black and White*
Certification: BPI: Silver

'Don't Go' (featuring Josh Kumra)
Year: 2011

Album: *Black and White*
Certification: BPI: Gold

'Forgiveness' (featuring Etta Bond)
Year: 2011
Album: *Black and White*

'Hush Little Baby' (featuring Ed Sheeran)
Year: 2012
Album: *Black and White*

'Blackout' (featuring Shakka)
Year: 2013

'Doing OK' (featuring Jacob Banks)
Year: 2013

'6 Words'
Year: 2014
Album: *Growing Over Life*

'Alright with Me' (featuring Anne-Marie and PRGRSHN)
Year: 2015

'Antwi'
Year: 2016
Album: *Growing Over Life*

'Liberation' (featuring KZ)
Year: 2016
Album: *Growing Over Life*

'All a Dream' (featuring Knox Brown)
Year: 2016
Album: *Growing Over Life*

'I.O.U.' (featuring Emeli Sandé)
Year: 2016
Album: *Growing Over Life*

'Open Conversation & Mark Duggan' (featuring Varren Wade, Bobii Lewis and Avelino)
Year: 2016
Album: *Growing Over Life*

'Whistle' (featuring Donae'o and Kojo Funds)
Year: 2017
Album: FR32

'Tell Me' (featuring Kojo Funds and Jahlani)
Year: 2017
Album: FR32

'His & Hers (Perspectives)'
Year: 2017
Album: FR32

'CYSAW' (with Knox Brown)
Year: 2018

'Mummy's Boy'
Year: 2019

As featured artist:

'Dancefloor' (DaVinChe featuring Wretch 32)
Year: 2010
Album: *Dancefloor EP*

'Hangover' (Starboy Nathan featuring Wretch 32)
Year: 2011
Album: *3D – Determination, Dedication, Desire*

'Teardrop' (as part of *The Collective*)
Year: 2011
Album: *3D – Determination, Dedication, Desire*

'Go In, Go Hard' (Angel featuring Wretch 32)
Year: 2012
Album: *About Time*

'Off with Their Heads' (Devlin featuring Wretch 32)
Year: 2012
Album: *A Moving Picture*

'Flatline' (Wilkinson featuring Wretch 32)
Year: 2016
Album: *Hypnotic*

'People' (Laura Mvula featuring Wretch 32)
Year: 2016
Album: *The Dreaming Room*

'Stop' (Alesha Dixon featuring Wretch 32)
Year: 2016
Album: *Do It for Love*

'Doubt' (Samm Henshaw featuring Wretch 32)
Year: 2018

Promotional singles

'Punctuation' (featuring Scorcher and Bashy)
Year: 2007
Album: *Teachers' Training Day*

'Be Cool' (featuring Wizzy Wow)
Year: 2008
Album: *Wretchrospective*

'Me and You'
Year: 2008
Album: *Wretchrospective*

'Ina Di Ghetto' (featuring Ghetts and Badness)
Year: 2008
Album: *Wretchrospective*

'Superhero'
Year: 2009

'Let's Go!'
Year: 2011

'Breathe (Sha La La)'
Year: 2012

'Blur'
Year: 2012

'Pop?'
Year: 2013

ACKNOWLEDGEMENTS

Thank you firstly to Akua Agyemfra, Zeon Richards and the management team.

Thank you to Ash Sarkar for her genius assistance and for allowing our minds to combine, and to Tom Avery and everyone at Penguin Random House.

Thank you to my family and friends, for their patience over the years.

And finally, a special thank you to Mr Henry, whose spirit lives on in every word I write.

TEXT
ACKNOWLEDGEMENTS

The author and publisher gratefully acknowledge the permission granted to reproduce the copyright material in this book. Every effort has been made to trace copyright holders and to obtain their permission. The publisher apologises for any errors or omissions and, if notified of any corrections, will make suitable acknowledgment in future reprints or editions of this book.

'Punctuation', 'Pisces', 'Fire In The Booth Part 3', 'Fire In The Booth Part 4', and 'Fire In The Booth Part 5' appear courtesy of Renowned Records. 'Hush Little Baby' and '6 Words' appear courtesy of Ministry of Sound Recordings Licensed by Wretch 32 Limited. 'Antwi', 'Cooked Food', 'His & Hers', 'Open Conversation & Mark Duggan' and 'Pisces' appear courtesy of Polydor Records, Licensed by Renowned Records. 'Upon Reflection' and 'Mummy's Boy' appear courtesy of Polydor Records.